# Letters from the Country

*1817*

**HARPER & ROW, PUBLISHERS,** New York
Cambridge, Hagerstown, Philadelphia, San Francisco,
London, Mexico City, São Paulo, Sydney

# Letters from the Country

## CAROL BLY

*To*

## *Alice Curtiss Sweeney*

The essays in this book originally appeared in *Preview* and the *Minnesota Monthly* between 1973 and 1979. They are reprinted by permission of the publisher, Minnesota Public Radio, Incorporated. Grateful acknowledgment is made for permission to reprint: Excerpt from "Flight Into Egypt" from W. H. Auden: *Collected Poems* by W. H. Auden, edited by Edward Menselson. Copyright 1944 and renewed 1972 by W. H. Auden. Reprinted by permission of Random House, Inc. Excerpts from *The Poetry of Robert Frost* edited by Edward Connery Lathem. Copyright 1923, © 1969 by Holt, Rinehart and Winston. Copyright 1936, 1951 by Robert Frost. Copyright © 1964 by Lesley Frost Ballantine. Reprinted by permission of Holt, Rinehart and Winston, Publishers. "In Distrust of Merits" from *Collected Poems of Marianne Moore*. Copyright 1944 and renewed 1972 by Marianne Moore. Reprinted by permission of Macmillan Publishing Co, Inc.

FIRST EDITION

*Designer: Gloria Adelson*

Library of Congress Cataloging in Publication Data

Bly, Carol.
    Letters from the country.

    "A series of short essays that Carol Bly wrote for the Minnesota monthly."
    1. Madison region, Minn.—Social life and customs—Addresses, essays, lectures. 2. Country life—Minnesota—Madison region—Addresses, essays, lectures. 3. Farm life—Minnesota—Madison region—Addresses, essays, lectures. 4. Madison region, Minn.—Rural conditions—Addresses, essays, lectures. I. Title.
F614.M14B58   1981      977.6'38      80-8194
ISBN 0-06-010357-4

81 82 83 84 85 10 9 8 7 6 5 4 3 2 1

# Contents

From the Lost Swede Towns   1

Getting Tired   8

Bruno Bettelheim: Three Ideas to Try in Madison,
    Minnesota   14

Forgiving Nixon in Madison, Minnesota   21

If a Thing Is Worth Doing, It's Worth Doing Badly   26

Enemy Evenings   32

Great Snows   40

Extended vs. Nuclear Families   45

Quietly Thinking Over Things at Christmas   51

To Unteach Greed   59

Rural Feelings: Starting in the Mailroom and Having to
    Stay There   64

Even Paranoids Have Enemies   69

Ways Out: I. Non-Resource People   74

Ways Out: II. We Are Sick of Bible Camp   80

Ways Out: III. The Way Out of Small-Town Niceness
    and Loneliness   84

Back at the Ranch, Small Dragons, Small Princesses   89

Brethren Too Least for Country Life   95

Turning Plowshares Back into Swords   101

The Last Person to Get a Grant   106

A Malaise for Followers   110

*A Gentle Education for Us All*   114

*Where Have All the Fifty-Five-Year-Olds Gone?*   120

*In the Same Bottle, a Different Genie*   126

*Our Class System*   132

*Chin Up in a Rotting Culture*   138

*A Mongoose Is Missing*   144

*To Be Rude and Hopeful Instead of Whining and
    Quitting*   150

*Koko and Wolfgang Amadeus in Rural Minnesota*   158

*The City Mouse, the Country Mouse, and the Overnight-
    Conference Mouse*   164

*The Sticking Place*   169

*Growing Up Expressive*   175

*The soul is constantly about to starve:
it cannot live on fun alone. If the soul
gets no other food, it will first tear
apart other creatures . . . then itself.*

—SELMA LÄGERLÖF

# From the Lost Swede Towns

Scott Fitzgerald remarked, somewhere toward the end of *Gatsby*, that his Middle West was the land of prep school boys' coming home at Christmas, their shouted inquiries in Chicago's Union Station, "Are you going to the Ordways'?" Fitzgerald said, very firmly, his Middle West was "not the wheat or the prairies or the lost Swede towns."

Lost Swede Towns Minnesota is where I live, and what these letters will be about. Our town of about 2,000—Madison—is 160 miles west of Minneapolis, well out of the range of Fitzgerald's readers or the Ordways' parties; out here, Groton and Exeter sound like seedcorn hybrids. This is the prairie country of the Louisiana Purchase, the endless, fainting fields, with the dusty rivers hooded by cottonwoods. As your eye sweeps this landscape you can see five or six farmers' "groves" (windbreaks around the farmhouses). At dawn and dusk the groves look like the silent, major ships of someone else's navy, standing well spaced, well out to sea.

It isn't really a country of "lost Swede towns"; the people are Norwegian and German in the main, but Fitzgerald struck true—there is a tremendous amount of loss in it.

When I came out here I thought it was just sexual loss. On my first visit, we drove in the evening. The bare bulbs were lighted in the passing farmyards. The barn lights were on for chores. I remember saying, How marvelous to think of night on this gigantic prairie—all the men and women making love in their safe houses guarded by the gloomy groves! Who wants to think of anyone making love in Los Angeles—but how great to think of it in these cozy farmhouses! The reply was: That's what *you* think!

Scandinavian-American sexual chill is a firm cliché, but what isn't so well known is that there is a restraint against *feeling in general*. There is restraint against enthusiasm ("real nice" is the adjective—not "marvelous"); there is restraint in grief ("real sober" instead of "heartbroken"); and always, always, restraint in showing your feelings, lest someone be drawn closer to you. This restraint was there with the first pioneers; the strong-minded Swiss-American writer Mari Sandoz, in describing her family's settling in Nebraska, called the newer, Scandinavian influx "mealy-mouthed." Mealy-mouthed means that when someone has stolen all four wheels off your car you say, "Oh, when I saw that car, with the wheels stripped off like that, I just thought ohhhhhhhh." "And that Vietnam War . . . well, it's just . . . well, it's just hard to know what to think!" Or "Watergate now. Well . . . it's just, well, that Watergate sure is something." If the topic is controversial, you seldom get a clear predicate to any sentence. In conversation, no predicate means the speaker has unconsciously decided not to give you that information after all.

Americans are always mourning that "the kids everywhere" have no feeling: that's another kind of phenomenon, but what you have to be clear about in Minnesota is that the Scandinavian-American doesn't feel because he doesn't *believe* in feeling. He is against it. It isn't only that he has watched too much television; his timidity and frigidity were there long before he was seduced by "The Edge of Night."

This summer *Charlotte's Web* made it to the Grand Theatre in Madison. We all flung ourselves into the movies because we'd had a drought, everyone had been anxious, and then it rained, and we celebrated. It rained well—not a rapid runoff rain that just grabs our topsoil and carries a lot of it to the Gulf of Mexico in five days, but a proper gardeners' rain, settling all night and all day, slowly crumbling the chunks near the corn stems, slowly slipping down past the thin things that are always lying around farms, spring tooth cultivators and loops of electric-fence wire flung around posts. After the movie the main street was full of Studebaker half-ton pickups collecting the farm kids, other cars gunning their engines in neutral, men in short sleeves dodging around in the light rain in the headlights. In the spooky light their arms looked black and the flesh didn't look as if it would be live and firm indefinitely. Some children who had seen the movie were crying, being hustled along by their mothers. We were all moved by the friendship of Char-lotte the spider and Wilbur the pig; our ears were full of E. B. White's final comment: "It is not often that someone comes along who is a true friend and a good writer. Charlotte was both." Then, suddenly, I heard two separate mothers tell their children: "Oh, for the love of goodness, it was just a movie!" and "Okay, okay, OKAY! You don't have to feel it *that* much."

This is the real death in our countryside, this not approving of feeling. It implies a disdain for literature, of course, since lit-erature so baldly champions feeling. Around town for a week after *Charlotte's Web* there were complaints that we had been promised "a cute movie" but the kids had cried. Actually, the producers did quite a lot to make it "a cute movie": they added 1940s songs of the "musical" kind; they removed humor, plot, and pathos; but lots of E. B. White still shone through.

I am interested in this phenomenon: the cute movie. We can all name things that happen when a whole segment of society, say, the lost Swede town part of society, fails to feel. They range from obeying murder orders at My Lai on down to Farm Bureau audiences sitting absolutely without smiles throughout a comedy routine. Addiction to meaningless entertainment (cute movies) isn't a tenth of it obviously, but it interests me because craving cute movies brings with it a craving for indifferent murder.

Nonfeeling people do not crave real death. They don't want to go out and beat up people, but they do have a very odd fascination for murders that can't possibly affect them. Movie producers know this, and since the 1960s have hiked the violence forward in the movie's playing time. No longer do you get an hour or so to empathize with Alan Ladd before someone shoots him; no longer do you know the characters before the violence enters; now you get some actor's face obliterated by shots while the credits are still being shown. This is the epitome of indifferent murder. No love, no hate, and no pity have been solicited of us. But then we didn't want any feeling solicited!

One of the various intelligent theories about the Vietnam War is that it was an unconscious replay of our murdering the American Indians. I sense another possibility: the Vietnam War was the chance of a lifetime to commit indifferent murder. Americans felt like killing where it meant nothing personally; a Southeast Asian farmer four thousand feet below one's wingtip filled the bill perfectly. It is his face that is destroyed during the movie credits.

A lingering, but unrealistic notion is that American society split its classes because of the Vietnam War, but the split, in fact, between Middle America (for our purpose here, Lost Swede Town America) and educated or enlightened America took place a long time ago. The cute movie syndrome is a good measure of it.

⋅ I first saw the cute movie syndrome in Duluth, in 1943. My gang of teenage girl friends wandered into an RAF movie. Once in, we were drawn into the Wellington's shadowy cockpit. Our faces were streaked with searchlights, and soon the prosaic girl next to me, in the perennial blue jeans and man's shirt with sleeves rolled, was replaced by my second pilot and the bomb aimer. One scene in particular affected me. Photographed from the ground, at first light of day, the crippled aircraft was flying home, over the English coastline. In the weak light everything looked ghostly and precious; the shore looked like the fine stretches between Folkestone and Dover. Then the plane sank lower and lower, over steep-pitched roofs and corbelled chimney tops. I had never thought before how fragile a village or a countryside is, how desperately close to destruction it can be, until I saw those chimney tops under the airplane. When adults talk about such feelings for one's country, we rather wish they'd got beyond facile patriotism by now. For a thirteen-year-old, however, the feeling that a country wants defending is nearly a spiritual experience.

In any case, the movie over, we clattered out and into a hot, bright bus for home. A few of the girls were annoyed we hadn't taken in a cute movie, but one voice suddenly rose over all the others: "All I can say is, if you're going to talk about the war and all that, boys are just never going to like you!"

A nice kaleidoscoping of appalling values, and the marriage of lightweight emotions to the ambitions of a sex object. If much of America has abandoned these stifling convictions, however, our lost Swede towns haven't.

Yet nobody wants to help our "Swede" to wake up. The twentieth-century way to look at the nonverbal, nonpassionate Midwesterner is to sneer. When someone asked Hemingway decades ago why he didn't write about normal Americans instead of idealists like his Robert Jordan, he replied, "Why should I write about people with broken legs?" Charles Reich's greening of America wasn't a genuine psychic revolution of affection because it was in large part merely a slap at the hardnosed classes. Reich's longhairs were johnnies come very lately onto that set: long ago, Fitzgerald saw how the Dobbs Ferry girls lifted their noses at the Lutheran syndrome; Hemingway's heroic dropouts despised wall-to-wall carpeting and nonorganic bread and the equivalent of snowmobile clubs long before the first hippy grieved because his mother wanted a blender.

The nonfeeling syndrome seems to work like this: (1) You repress the spontaneous feelings in life; (2) but spontaneous feelings are the source of enjoyment; so (3) enjoyment must be artificially applied from without (cute movies). (4) You repress your innate right to evaluate events and people, but (5) energy comes from making your own evaluations and then acting on them, so (6) therefore your natural energy must be replaced by indifferent violence.

The churches in Minnesota have had their part in vitiating the natural energy of people. Most of rural Minnesota go to church regularly, yet nearly never get a sermon on Jesus' turning the tables on the moneychangers. They absolutely never get a sermon on Saul's having failed to obliterate the Amalekites so that Samuel has to cut Agag, the Amalekite king, to pieces in front of Saul, to give him an idea what the Lord had in mind; they absolutely never get a sermon on St. Stephen's being stoned while Saul, later to become St. Paul, approved. The pastors, themselves tottering around in an emotional sleepwalk, don't face the crises of their faith. They do not make themselves answer: was Hosea right in his incredible and violent hostility to women? Is Cardinal Spellman right in saying the 25th Infantry carried the cross of Christ in Vietnam? Since the pastors lack such energy—to think, and feel, and commit themselves—the people are left with no example of Christ's energy. No castle was ever well guarded by sleepwalkers, and certainly no Kingdom of the Spirit can rise up in the hearts of somnambulants.

What is crueler, however, is that it is now commercially practicable to keep our lost Swede asleep. One villain in this is the Shakespeare-in-the-Streets troupe of Minneapolis. A few years ago they took around to our towns, among them Madison, a *Hamlet* in which the characters were hashed (Hamlet appeared double: one white, one black), the plot changed into a spaced-out pas de mille choreography, and the soliloquies were done in a kind of black stomp. Having removed all the real energy of the play then, cute movie things had to be added. A dead chicken was thrown around, Polonius got kicked hard in the shins, and so on. The manager told me, "Oh we did it on purpose, because the common people [*sic*] wouldn't like it straight."

This past winter, the children's theatre group from the University of Minnesota brought to Madison a program of four Hans Christian Andersen fairy tales. They were excellent—beautiful. Still, they turned the Ugly Duckling into a kind of black-face humor piece, even done with what were ominously close to fake-black accents. They made the Ugly Duckling, in effect, a cute show. This meant that our lost Swede Minnesotan, who hadn't read the original Andersen, didn't get to hear Andersen on the injustice of early selection, the sorrow of the eccentric child, or the heartbreaking discovery of one's true element late in life.

Educated Americans spent the summer of 1973 sneering at Middle America for turning off their televisions during the Watergate hearings. It is true, in the beauty shops, the TV was turned off because of "that Watergate." But who tried sincerely to show the lady in rollers that it is strengthening, not weakening, to feel what's happening in the United States? Too many of our intellectuals have left the Swede by the roadside.

The billboard just south of Madison on U.S. 75 now reads: "Don't just sit there—Be a Navy man." If all feeling is dead, those are the choices: feeling nothing, motivated by nothing—or join an organization which specializes in indifferent killing.

Our countryside has inherited not Grieg, not Ibsen, not Rölvaag—but just sitting there, cute movies, and when boredom gets bad enough, joining the Navy.

The problem of people's not feeling is very serious, and I haven't any answers. But I think we should get onto this issue now, and we should buck each other's ideas back and forth. Selma Lägerlöf, who was emphatically a very live Swede, was right in warning that the soul cannot live on fun alone . . . it will kill. We know that now.

September 1973

# Getting Tired

The men have left a gigantic 6600 combine a few yards from our grove, at the edge of the stubble. For days it was working around the farm; we heard it on the east, later on the west, and finally we could see it grinding back and forth over the windrows on the south. But now it has been simply squatting at the field's edge, huge, tremendously still, very professional, slightly dangerous.

We all have the correct feelings about this new combine: this isn't the good old farming where man and soil are dusted together all day; this isn't farming a poor man can afford, either, and therefore it further threatens his hold on the American "family farm" operation. We have been sneering at this machine for days, as its transistor radio, amplified well over the engine roar, has been grinding up our silence, spreading a kind of shrill ghetto evening all over the farm.

But now it is parked, and after a while I walk over to it and climb up its neat little John-Deere-green ladder on the left. Entering the big cab up there is like coming up into a large ship's bridge on visitors' day—heady stuff to see the inside workings of a huge operation like the Queen Elizabeth II. On the other hand I feel left out, being only a dumbfounded passenger. The combine cab has huge windows flaring wider at the top; they lean forward over the ground, and the driver sits so high behind the glass in its rubber moldings it is like a movie-set spaceship. He has obviously come to dominate the field, whether he farms it or not.

The value of the 66 is that it can do anything, and to change it from a combine into a cornpicker takes one man about half an hour, whereas most machine conversions on farms take several men a half day. It frees its owner from a lot of monkeying.

Monkeying, in city life, is what little boys do to clocks so they never run again. In farming it has two quite different meanings. The first is small side projects. You monkey with poultry, unless you're a major egg handler. Or you monkey with ducks or geese. If you have a very small milk herd, and finally decide that prices plus state regulations don't make your few Holsteins worthwhile, you "quit monkeying with them." There is a hidden dignity in this word: it precludes mention of money. It lets the wife of a very marginal farmer have a conversation with a woman who may be helping her husband run fifteen hundred acres. "How you coming with those geese?" "Oh, we've been real disgusted. We're thinking of quitting monkeying with them." It saves her having to say, "We lost our shirts on those darn geese."

The other meaning of monkeying is wrestling with and maintaining machinery, such as changing heads from combining to cornpicking. Farmers who cornpick the old way, in which the corn isn't shelled automatically during picking in the field but must be elevated to the top of a pile by belt and then shelled, put up with some monkeying.

Still, cornpicking and plowing is a marvelous time of the year on farms; one of the best autumns I've had recently had a few days of fieldwork in it. We were outside all day, from six in the morning to eight at night—coming in only for noon dinner. We ate our lunches on a messy truck flatbed. (For city people who don't know it: *lunch* isn't a noon meal; it is what you eat out of a black lunch pail at 9 A.M. and 3 P.M. If you offer a farmer a cup of coffee at 3:30 P.M. he or she is likely to say, "No thanks, I've already had lunch.") There were four of us hired to help—a couple to plow, Celia (a skilled farmhand who worked steady for our boss), and me. Lunch was always two sandwiches of white commercial bread with luncheon meat, and one very generous piece of cake-mix cake carefully wrapped in Saran Wrap. (I never found anyone around here self-conscious about using Saran Wrap when the Dow Chemical Company was also making napalm.)

It was very pleasant on the flatbed, squinting out over the yellow picked cornstalks—each time we stopped for lunch, a larger part of the field had been plowed black. We fell into the easy psychic habit of farmworkers: admiration of the boss. "Ja, I see he's buying one of those big 4010s," someone would say. We always perked up at inside information like that. Or "Ja," as the woman hired steady told us, "he's going to plow the home fields first this time, instead of the other way round." We temporary help were impressed by that, too. Then, with real flair, she brushed a crumb of luncheon meat off her jeans, the way you would make sure to flick a gnat off spotless tennis whites. It is the true feminine touch to brush a crumb off pants that are encrusted with Minnesota Profile A heavy loam, many swipes of SAE 40 oil, and grain dust.

All those days, we never tired of exchanging information on how *he* was making out, what *he* was buying, whom *he* was going to let drive the new tractor, and so on. There is always something to talk about with the other hands, because farming is genuinely absorbing. It has the best quality of work: nothing else seems real. And everyone doing it, even the cheapest helpers like me, can see the layout of the whole—from spring work, to cultivating, to small grain harvest, to cornpicking, to fall plowing.

The second day I was promoted from elevating corncobs at the corn pile to actual plowing. Hour after hour I sat up there on the old Alice, as she was called (an Allis-Chalmers WC that looked rusted from the Flood). You have to sit twisted part way around, checking that the plowshares are scouring clean, turning over and dropping the dead crop and soil, not clogging. For the first two hours I was very political. I thought about what would be good for American farming—stronger marketing organizations, or maybe a law like the Norwegian Odal law, preventing the breaking up of small farms or selling them to business interests. Then the sun got high, and each time I reached the headlands area at the field's end I dumped off something else, now my cap, next my jacket, finally my sweater.

Since the headlands are the last to be plowed, they serve as a field road until the very end. There are usually things parked there—a pickup or a corn trailer—and things dumped—my warmer clothing, our afternoon lunch pails, a broken furrow wheel someone picked up.

By noon I'd dropped all political interest, and was thinking only: how unlike this all is to Keats's picture of autumn, a "season of mists and mellow fruitfulness." This gigantic expanse of horizon, with everywhere the easy growl of tractors, was simply teeming with extrovert energy. It wouldn't calm down for another week, when whoever was lowest on the totem pole would be sent out to check a field for dropped parts or to drive away the last machines left around.

The worst hours for all common labor are the hours after noon dinner. Nothing is inspiring then. That is when people wonder how they ever got stuck in the line of work they've chosen for life. Or they wonder where the cool Indian smoke of secrets and messages began to vanish from their marriage. Instead of plugging along like a cheerful beast working for me, the Allis now smelled particularly gassy. To stay awake I froze my eyes onto an indented circle in the hood around the gas cap. Someone had apparently knocked the screw cap fitting down into the hood, so there was a moat around it. In this moat some overflow gas leapt in tiny waves. Sometimes the gas cap was a castle, this was the moat; sometimes it was a nuclear-fission plant, this was the horrible hot-water waste. Sometimes it was just the gas cap on the old Alice with the spilt gas bouncing on the hot metal.

Row after row. I was stupefied. But then around 2:30 the shadows appeared again, and the light, which had been dazing and white, grew fragile. The whole prairie began to gather itself for the cool evening. All of a sudden it was wonderful to be plowing again, and when I came to the field end, the filthy jackets and the busted furrow wheel were just benign mistakes: that is, if it chose to, the jacket could be a church robe, and the old wheel could be something with some pride to it, like a helm. And I felt the same about myself: instead of being someone with a half interest in literature and a half interest in farming doing a half-decent job plowing, I could have been someone desperately needed in Washington or Zurich. I drank my three o'clock coffee joyously, and traded the other plowman a Super-Valu cake-mix lemon cake slice for a Holsum baloney sandwich because it had garlic in it.

By seven at night we had been plowing with headlights for an hour. I tried to make up games to keep going, on my second wind, on my third wind, but labor is labor after the whole day of it; the mind refuses to think of ancestors. It refuses to pretend the stalks marching up to the right wheel in the spooky light are men-at-arms, or to imagine a new generation coming along. It doesn't care. Now the Republicans could have announced a local meeting in which they would propose a new farm program whereby every farmer owning less than five hundred acres must take half price for his crop, and every farmer owning more than a thousand acres shall receive triple price for his crop, and I was so tired I wouldn't have shown up to protest.

A million hours later we sit around in a daze at the dining-room table, and nobody says anything. In low, courteous mutters we ask for the macaroni hotdish down this way, please. Then we get up in ones and twos and go home. Now the farm help are all so tired we *are* a little like the various things left out on the headlands—some tools, a jacket, someone's thermos top—used up for that day. Thoughts won't even stick to us any more.

Such tiredness must be part of farmers' wanting huge machinery like the Deere 6600. That tiredness that feels so good to the occasional laborer and the athlete is disturbing to a man destined to it eight months of every year. But there is a more hidden psychology in the issue of enclosed combines versus open tractors. It is this: one gets too many impressions on the open tractor. A thousand impressions enter as you work up and down the rows: nature's beauty or nature's stubbornness, politics, exhaustion, but mainly the feeling that all this repetition—last year's cornpicking, this year's cornpicking, next year's cornpicking—is taking up your lifetime. The mere repetition reveals your eventual death.

When you sit inside a modern combine, on the other hand, you are so isolated from field, sky, all the real world, that the brain is dulled. You are not sensitized to your own mortality. You aren't sensitive to anything at all.

This must be a common choice of our mechanical era: to hide from life inside our machinery. If we can hide from life in there, some idiotic part of the psyche reasons, we can hide from death in there as well.

# Bruno Bettelheim:
# Three Ideas to Try
# in Madison, Minnesota

It is exhilarating to spend a few days thinking about the ideas of Bruno Bettelheim,* not just because he has such energy and moral genius, but because he is so out of style at the moment. The attention, and certainly the affections, of the liberal intelligentsia are somewhere else, and I feel private and quiet among Bettelheim's findings, instead of feeling like one of a cheering crowd at the arena. There is no distraction.

I expect Bettelheim owes his unpopularity to the fact that he is such a mixed bag: he gets off some of the coarsest censures of young people, leftists, and women that you can come across. He is good and out of fashion. What I like and honor in him is his constant work on *decency*. In a decade given to opening up the unconscious almost as an end in itself, Bettelheim still goes on working on decency between people, decency based square-

* Dr. Bettelheim has written many books. I've taken some of his ideas here from *The Informed Heart, The Empty Fortress,* and some recent newspaper interviews.

ly on the moral well-being within each person. He calls this moral well-being "individual autonomy." Roughly, it means that no matter how sensibly some insane or cruel proposition is presented to you, you make up your own mind that it is not acceptable, and you do not do the insane or cruel thing.

Applying Bruno Bettelheim's perspective to life in rural Minnesota means taking ideas learned *in great straits* (in the concentration camp at Dachau and later, in the Orthogenic School of the University of Chicago, where he treated autistic children) and deliberately using them *in little straits*. I commend this idea because the countryside, despite its apparent culture lag, is doomed to be wrecked in the mass culture just as surely as the cities are being wrecked. We need major thinking, but our habit is to listen only to the local prophets—mild-mannered provincial professionals living among us, regional poets with their evident faith in nature, local administrators of community education projects. Our habit is to listen to those nearby who are affable and low-key. They can't save our personalities, though, any better than fervent quilt making can save our artistic nature or Solarcaine can set a broken leg.

Certainly life in western Minnesota must be about as untroublesome as life anywhere in the twentieth century. It is only luck; we haven't ourselves done anything, psychically or morally, to protect us from the coarsening of life that comes with more population. We are all set to become "mass men"—or at least we have no proofs that we won't give way to impersonal relations, increasing rudeness, increasing distrust, ill-temper while queuing up for everything from tennis courts to funeral reservations. Bettelheim's ideas—and I've chosen three of them to think about—have to do with how to keep the self from succumbing to the mass state. The three ideas are (1) replacing the feeling of "business as usual" with crisis thinking, (2) forcing ourselves to have a sense of time in our lives, and (3) understanding the power of negative thinking.

Even when the Germans began arresting Jews in the 1930s,

many of the Jews refused to leave Germany because the aura of their possessions—the rooms, the rugs, the paintings—gave them a sense of normalcy in things: they'd projected some of themselves into these objects around them, so if the objects were still there, surely everything was usual? What they needed to do was to switch to *crisis thinking:* they needed to say to themselves, "This is *not* business as usual. We must run away at night, or join the Underground, or separate and plan to meet in Switzerland."

Bettelheim says we must speak or fight, whichever is called for, at the *first moment of our anxiety*. National Socialism looked like "business as usual" in 1932 and 1933; by 1934 it was too late. The Gestapo's intention to terrify eighty million Germans through the constant threat of the camps was published long before they actually did it, but few paid attention. *Mein Kampf* should have been lots of warning: very few people took it seriously. So Bettelheim suggests we must ask ourselves at every other moment, Is this business as usual? Is this a crisis? Is it O.K. to go on just maintaining my life today, or must I act in a political way? So here are some questions we can ask in rural Minnesota:

1. Should the President be impeached? Now is the moment of our anxiety over his crookedness: should we impeach? If not, is there something else we should be doing? Is it really O.K. just to be sitting here?
2. Is TV watching turning our children into mass men or is it not? Many parents in Madison have said explicitly they think TV watching is bad for their children, but only two families I know of have got rid of the set. Somehow, the course of each day's activity disperses the parents' anxiety. Since they do not act in the moment of anxiety, then the children go on dully taking in the commercials and the vulgarity of feeling and another week goes by, a year goes by, and the day after tomorrow, or perhaps it was

yesterday, the children are eighteen and they have been watching television for seventeen years. They saw eighteen thousand murders by the time they were fourteen (according to *TV Generation*, by Gerald Loomey), and all the while the parents sincerely felt that TV watching was bad for them.

3. Is the American diet really "well balanced" as the Department of Agriculture would have us believe, or have the grain-milling companies (who systematically began degerminating all wheat flour on the market in the second decade of the century) caused a deficiency of Vitamin E (and other vitamins as well) which is responsible for the multiplying incidence of certain diseases and a sharp rise in fatalities from them? Does it mean anything that in the pamphlets given 4-H children, telling them how to make bread, the picture credits are nearly all to those very grain-milling companies?

A sense of time warns that now is the time; it is not business as usual. Thinking of time leads to the second idea of Bettelheim's I'd like to bring in: a sense of *time left*. The Gestapo cleverly realized that if you never know *when* something will happen, such as the release of a prisoner from camp or the end of a slave-work detail, you can't organize your own thoughts. A crude example that comes to my mind is the dilemma of a runner; if he doesn't know how many laps remain, how shall he husband his diminishing strength? When shall he make his final spurt? Christianity feels the sense of *time left* so strongly that the Church teaches that you must regard every moment as your last, so that you will make the final, mortal spurt always. But mass society, which tends to make people relaxed and low-key and unambitious, encourages a slack time sense. Here's an example from my town.

As soon as a Madison girl marries she will be asked to join most if not all of the following groups:

1. A circle of church women
2. The large Ladies' Aid, which meets monthly.
3. A homemakers' group
4. An auxiliary of the American Legion or the VFW
5. Mrs. Jaycees
6. A study club (Federated Women's Clubs of America)
7. Women's—or couples'—bridge club

I have omitted community groups that do useful work, such as teaching released-time school, or shampooing at the Home, filling hospital bird-feeding stations, or working in the hospital auxiliary. These projects are self-justifying.

If the young woman doesn't say to herself: I am twenty-five and in seventy years I will probably be dead, she is likely to join the organizations listed. If she has a sense of *time left*, however, she may ask the right questions: How much of my life do I want to spend in solitude? Most women in town also drink coffee with two or more other women at 10 A.M. and at 3 P.M. every day. This means another three hours a day of time spent in idle social intercourse. Yet, whenever we ask these young women if they think they might on their deathbeds regret this casual frittering away of time, they grin and say, "Oh, let's not be morbid now!"

Still, forty-five-year-old women do start dropping out of the artificially structured social life in Madison: people who have dazedly accepted belonging to clubs for twenty years now choose to topple into their own inner lives instead. They simply have finally learned a sense of *time left*—and the tragedy of it is that a spiritually dormant society ever allowed them to waste twenty years.

A few years ago we had a constantly cheerful minister in town; no one was less apprehensive than he. He wasn't nervous about the hydrogen bomb and he wasn't nervous about our participation in the Vietnam War. Then he became critically ill, and upon recovery he preached for an entire winter the first serious, thoughtful sermons of his life, or at least of his life here. Any number of people complained that the sermons had gone morbid and "negative." They hadn't. He simply had learned a sense of *time left*.

Complaints about "negative" sermons bring me to the third of Bettelheim's ideas: the usefulness of negative or critical thinking. Bettelheim objects to everyone's seizing on Anne Frank's "All men are basically good." He argues that they wish to derive comfort from their admiration of her positive attitude under such awful circumstances, instead of feeling uncomfortable with the truth—which is that men are basically good and they are basically bad. They can be ghastly. Stanley Milgram's *Obedience to Authority* describes an experiment in which subjects were directed to "administer pain" to people strapped in chairs in the next room who were visible through the window. The subjects believed that the dials they operated gave pain whenever the people strapped to the chair failed to learn a given piece of information. Some of the subjects repeatedly turned the dial to the "danger" markings on the machine. They were sadistic without even noticing. If we keep in mind such left-handed inhumanity—Americans just obeying orders—and then repeat to ourselves Anne Frank's remark about men being basically good, we are irritated: näiveté, which ever wants to preserve its artless high, is ignoring rank cruelty. Positive thinking is that kind of näiveté. People who practice or commend it are interested in feeling no pain and in preserving a high. Sometimes a whole culture wishes to preserve this high: then its art and doctrines turn not into positive thinking but into positive pretending.

We haven't got a Germany here, but we do have a TV space-selling society. Hence a generation has grown up on mostly happy, bland, evasive propaganda. No wonder this beastly positive thinking, which means positive *pretending*, has become the crutch of church and club. The other day a clergyman told me he "preferred to think of the Ten Commandments as positive, not negative." Marvelous! What is the *positive* way not to commit adultery? How do you *positively* not covet your neighbor's husband? How do you *positively* not steal from the Klein National Bank?

Bettelheim noted that, when he first wrote his interpretations of the concentration camps, his readers told him they felt "a strange relief," gruesome as the subject was. No matter how oppressive the facts, facing them, calling evil evil, safeguards our personalities.

Why read a set of ideas based on imprisonment in Dachau in 1938? When I first began reading Bettelheim years ago I had the uncanny sensation he was handing me a beautifully thought-out set of bright tools, to keep me (or anyone) in one piece. He showed a way not to sit around absent-mindedly while a gross society raveled away decency like a yarn ball. As much as anyone I've read, Bettelheim helps us not to be wrecked. It takes affection to keep preventing wrecks, and saving people already wrecked. You feel this tough affection in his ideas.

Autumn 1973

# Forgiving Nixon in Madison, Minnesota

As more and more of the President's offenses against the people are revealed, it is interesting that ordinary citizens are more and more advised to "forgive the President."

The issue mysteriously becomes: "Am I good enough to forgive the President?" Ministers as well as editorial writers have taken up this view; they freely tell their congregations they must forgive the President or it will tear up the nation. The prominent Korean America-lover, Pastor Moon, has delivered the same advice.

Two things are simply wrong about the forgiveness phenomenon. The first, I think, is that the problem is not whether individual Americans forgive the President or not: the problem is not of personal morality or psychology, but of practical justice. Does the State of California get back what the President failed to pay in income tax? Will the United States, somehow or other, recover monies channeled to the President's personal properties and comforts? Will the humane programs so brutally curtailed—cancer research, mental health programs, housing programs, dozens of others—be returned to the staffs who worked on them and to those American people who desperately need them? For us to worry about whether a few millions of citizenry "forgive" the President or not is a psychic luxury—and where good men allow themselves psychic luxuries, evil will prevail.

The other wrong-headed aspect of the forgive-Nixon syndrome, I think, has to do specifically with small-town life. In western Minnesota it is correct to forgive Nixon. It is also correct to pity him. The current correct remark to make, in social or business situations, is: "I'm not for or against the President—I just feel sorry for him." This is the layman's parallel to the cleric's "I can find it in my heart to forgive him."

Why is pity ordered up, among ordinary people, for a man who can buy out Madison's Sixth Avenue with his right hand tied in his pocket, and to whom this whole question of pity or forgiveness would appear ludicrous? The answer is, I think, that the people have so little connection with national life—they read so little news, and such a small part of their conversations has anything to do with American politics—that they really have to cast about for some response to have to Nixon. They feel they ought to respond somehow, and since clergymen are expected to lead the comment on ethical issues, the rural clergy have carried the whole Nixon treachery into the church camp, to be illuminated by clerical conventions such as forgiveness, pity, tolerance, etc. If county judges had one one-hundredth the profile in rural Minnesota that the ministerium have, the Nixon episode would be considered in terms of justice, crookedness, equity, paying it off, etc. It just happens the church got hold of this issue.

Whenever people have no particular relationship to a subject, they generally project something onto it from things they *do* know about. For example, most rural Minnesotans have no particular feelings about apartheid in South Africa—yet they are pressured into expressing strong opinions. It stymies the ego. What should I say? What am I supposed to think? What kind of place is Johannesburg anyway? So one casts about for something to say that sounds authoritative enough so one won't sound like a fool. A news photo stirs in the memory: someone was hit by a South African policeman. It gives a clue for an acceptable opinion to have. "Frankly, what we need is law and order" is the comment, then. It has a manly simplicity, and a familiarity: it must be all right to think it about South Africa. Basically, Watergate was met with the same psychometrics: "The man needs forgiveness."

On the surface such a response to national events is pathetic. Under the surface it is dangerous. It hides the repressed resentment that powerful people get away with stealing from the public, and little people do not. I know that if I am caught breaking into the Union 76 station, Sheriff Fields is not going to ask me to rob the till ever more slowly until my act of theft is phased out. I also know that I will not be allowed to bank my loot, while large numbers of the American people are instructed to forgive me and pity me. Therefore, I feel the terrific injustice of the President's situation compared with mine.

But in a small town rage against a U.S. President is no more acceptable than anti-war protest. By and large, a forgiving and relaxed attitude rather than an angry and tense one is the acceptable stance. Although many hard-working people in Madison and other towns and on farms have grief making ends meet because of inflation, and they are honorably trying to use ten gallons per week or less of gas, and are adulterating their children's meals with Hamburger Helper, they are still not free, not *really free*, to complain about Nixon over coffee because it isn't acceptable. So the anger circles around inside the people, where it turns into a generalized sort of hostility that breaks surface here or there.

Rural towns are already psychically exhausted anyway, just from keeping the correct persona going. (This is hardly a new idea. The best books I've read that touch on it are *Village in the Vaucluse*, by Laurence Wylie, *A Small Town in a Mass Society*, by Arthur Vidich and Joseph Bensman, and Ronald Blyth's *Akenfield*.) It is exhausting, purely exhausting, to drink coffee together twice a day (at 10 A.M. and 3 P.M.—men to the Pantry and the Royal, housewives to one another's homes) and never express a divergent opinion. Recently I frankly wanted to know some school gossip, but the friend I went to for it said, "Oh no, you see I'd be the last to know anyway, because I coffee with some of the teachers and school things are controversial so that's taboo." Surely it must vitiate the spirit to spend two and three-quarter hours a day for between forty and fifty years without speaking one's mind.

What such repression of feelings, whether joyful or furious ones, finally leads to is not real pity for Nixon at all, much less justice for Nixon and pity for the United States. What it leads to is self-pity. Here is an approximate sort of listing of the Correct Attitudes toward Watergate and Nixon, from June to December of 1973, showing how the self-pity gradually mounts:

*June:* "It's just hard to know what to believe."

*July:* "They sure like digging up all this dirt, and it doesn't do any good that I can see."

*August:* "I wish they'd just get it over with, one way or the other, just to get it over with."

*September:* "I feel sorry for Nixon. It isn't just him either, it's the whole system, and not just the Republicans either, but he's taking the rap for all the rest of them."

*October:* "I feel sorry for Nixon. I wish they'd hurry up and get off his back. If he did it they should do something about it or otherwise shut up about it and get off his back."

*November:* "I feel sorry for Nixon. If they're going to impeach him I wish they'd do it and if they're not going to I wish they'd stop talking about it all the time."

*December:* "I feel sorry for Nixon. I think the whole thing ought to be settled one way or the other because it is tearing up the whole United States, it's just tearing up the country."

By and large the speaker doesn't care how it is settled, just so it *is*, and he or she can return to private life. But here is the snag: if you express only those judgments and emotions which are *correct* for your town, you haven't really got any private life.

Where there is no private life there is no enthusiasm, and there is little enough enthusiasm in our towns. The adults spend hours and hours in desultory conversation inside their houses, even after a new snowfall, even in the summer evenings; the teenagers' blanched expressions often suggest they don't hope to live with any passion. Surely the crawling pace at which the ladies' clubs labor through *Robert's Rules* and the thousands and thousands of times in both men's and women's organizations that the chairman finally must drawl, "Well . . . if there isn't any discussion then . . . I guess, we might as well vote. . . ." Surely these cry for change.

Psychic change may well be impossible, but I think we ought to try one idea after another. For starters, we could teach children of eight and older, systematically, in school, church, and home, to say to themselves many times a day: That is my *good* reason for having done that; but what was my *real* reason? This is my *good* attitude toward (Nixon or anyone else): what is my *real* attitude? If we could learn to check for and recognize the difference between good and real, to slough off front, we might free energy for real and joyful gratitude or for real and heartfelt fury.

Rural Minnesota life looks natural to people living in it. It seems natural to be this way—impersonal, guarded, hiding thoughts, hiding feelings, edgy about the neighbors. Yet it isn't natural: surely neither of the Covenants was made to perpetuate such lackluster soldiering. And it seems a shocker to me that thousands of people who are so honest that you can leave your car keys around in their towns should have been instructed pity for Nixon.

# If a Thing Is Worth Doing,
# It's Worth Doing Badly

The year of Gustav Holst's centenary is a good time to quote his marvelous encouragement to music lovers: if it's worth doing, it's worth doing badly. To Holst it meant that the Lilys and Freds of the choir of Thaxted Church in Essex, England, had a right to work out the breves and semibreves in Palestrina, and sing them on the great days, why not? To me it means that every town in Minnesota that wants to ought to go ahead and have its theatre, hire a painter-in-residence, and very definitely let the B-Band trumpets screech through the Handel at Christmas.

We are getting regional arts organizations all around the state now, but to make real use of them (whether of their expertise, equipment, or grants) a town has to have its local structure. I would like to offer some ideas about such local structures. First, I'd like to do a quick run through the pitfalls to be avoided.

One is the mistake that colors New England art scenes: the pasting of urban culture onto the countryside. A *New Yorker* cartoon feelingly notes "the goddam summer people," who trot from one stock-theatre town to another, from Connecticut to Maine. Their dozens of performances of *The Importance of Being Earnest* and *The Telephone* are as useful to the local people as a smear of pâté de anything on a peanut-butter sandwich. We're safer in Minnesota: we haven't Kennebunkport on the one side and the East Seventies on the other; there's natural traffic between St. Paul, Minneapolis, and Duluth, and Kandiyohi and Cannon Falls and Grand Rapids.

Also, we seem to be escaping the ladies' friends-of-the-arts syndrome, at least out here, probably because the state's funding groups are also *thinking* groups: they try to bring out what's natively here. When the Minnesota State Arts Council's "Poets Outloud" turn up they arrive in town as seed poets only. In Madison, in fact, they were lucky to get a stanza in edgewise at their own scheduled reading. In Minneota, the local Icelandic-American troops even read poems in Icelandic, and incidentally, did the advance publicity of the program themselves.

After the pitfall of pasting culture onto the countryside, the next one is failing to insist on excellence. We must do our plays and write our poems ourselves, but we have to see and hear what is great. The reply that if people want what is great they can drive in to the Guthrie Theatre in Minneapolis once in a while is a lie. The people can't drive in to the Guthrie; it costs too much, and the parents won't take their children anyway. We need to hire the great companies to come out to us: the St. Paul Chamber Orchestra, the Children's Theatre Company; all the people doing beautiful work in performance are desperately needed. Christ's opinion was very firm about this, said another way: "The laborer is worthy of his hire." Spiritual work is worth doing, and our towns need to be willing to pay for it.

On this point, I would like to paraphrase Ruth Humleker, who served as Acting Director at the State Arts Council and has written first-rate remarks on the "Hockey Syndrome." Humleker asks, when Minnesota fathers want their boys to grow up to be good hockey players, what do they do? They provide the handsomest equipment, the best teachers, whom they pay, *cheerfully*, and they take the boys to the best games whenever they can afford it. They do not hire semi-attentive grad students to teach their kids hockey on the side, for the dollars; they do not take their kids to watch Hockey-in-the-Streets, in which case the game is played without skates to make it simpler. But in the arts the same parents (and the same school boards) are too often content with (1) no instruction, (2) dispirited instruction and (3) mediocre goals in the first place. So the fighting proposition behind Humleker's Hockey Syndrome is: let's get the *very best*—at least once in a while.

The third and last pitfall I'd like to describe before offering some detours around them is self-consciousnees. There is nothing to beat the self-consciousness you feel when you put on your first play in a town that has never seen a play and never wanted one so far as anyone can tell, and what's more, is of two minds on whether or not plays will (1) make everybody immoral and (2) introduce communism. You have all that to deal with, plus your own conviction that this first play isn't being very well acted or very well directed—which in my experience has been a sound conviction. It is all very well when people jolly you up by saying you fell on your face instead of your backside, but the fact is there is excruciating embarrassment in a bad play, a messy poem, or even smudged rosemaling.

Here are some ideas for art in the countryside: first, it helps *not* to have a free-standing art or culture club. It works out very well, on the other hand, to ask the local Chamber of Commerce or City Council or other civic group to set up an arts committee as a part of their organization. They won't sneer. Chambers of Commerce are weary of their image as the ugly Americans forever coming on with mindless, upbeat chauvinism. Their national organization has been trying for some years to "broaden the concept." When a Chamber initiates an arts committee, it need have only one Chamber member on it and need report only quarterly with the other committees. Being part of the Chamber makes these committee workers less artsy and less egotistical than usual, I think; but better still, it means the performances they offer are gifts—like something in a promotional scheme—instead of cultural events.

In our town we found we could defeat self-consciousness by offering children's plays, put on by adults, as a gift to the children of the town from the grownups. We timed the first ones for Christmas, when gifts seem natural. The next helpful thing we found was to work with classic material. If a play is going to be middle-ground producing and middle-ground acting, you are still doing something worth doing if you do real art. We chose regular fairy tales; we did not rewrite them into fashionable psychodrama or into musicals. We kept the witch screeching and full of death, and the roof of the gingerbread house was real cookies, thanks to the bakery.

It's a good thing to follow Holst's encouragement to do amateur performing, but the work-of-art in question still needs full respect. No Hockey-in-the-Streets. In any case, the Jung and Marie-Louise von Franz theories tell us the psychic meaning in the old fairy tales is tremendously applicable and telling. Best not rewrite it. The other reason fairy tales are good is that the adults in town know them and enjoy recovering for a half hour their old dream world. Recently we had a full house watching the school counselor as the Troll, and the county judge as the Biggest Billy Goat Gruff, and the adults were at least as appreciative as the children. (Jungian philosopher Marie-Louise von Franz, for those who haven't read her ideas, would say that what we need is to see our "shadow." Therefore, what better example of *shadow* than to watch a judge known for courteousness and patience and disinterested decisions act out, full force, pure senseless aggression, bad temper for its own sake, disgusting *puer aeternus* willfulness, and finally, the spectacle of physical might defeating property rights, namely, as in The Three Billy Goats Gruff? It was gorgeous.)

Another reason for using civic groups as art cores instead of arts clubs is that you can involve more people from a wider background. If such a group puts on plays for four years, about 150 people will have been brought into working on drama. I think that not less than four times a year, every town paper should carry an advertisement asking more people interested in any art to come forward. It should be clear that there isn't any one group doing all this; there is the one public group sponsoring, but hundreds of different people are performing. If this announcement isn't made quarterly, in a town of 2,500 or less the arts descend the slick slope into the hands of an art élite. Then these people become, as they rather hoped to, a kind of "goddam summer people" as opposed to the regular people.

A last idea: maybe it would be possible for town groups to *compose* more art than they do. For example, commercial movies are often made on the story-doctoring committee principle: some people meet regularly and make up the plot. Between sessions a writer writes it all down. A town might advertise in the paper that all those interested should make up a *novel about their own town* on the same principle. Then these people would hammer out their views: what aspects of their life together should they bring out? what kinds of characters should they make up to carry the story? what kind of a story would it be a joy to write? which actual people in the town, really living there, should be worked into the novel? They could meet once a week all one winter, with a writer writing it down for them. This would not produce excellence, but it would provide self-observation, which isn't general in southwestern Minnesota in any case, and it would certainly provide respect for good plot writers like Dickens and Louisa May Alcott and Dorothy Sayers and Jane Austen. The group that worked together on something like that together would never forget it. Esprit de corps in those towns isn't general either; this would help. It's possible, of course, that the idea is totally ridiculous.

The Holst quotation does set us free to try our wings, but it presupposes earnestness: that is, the "thing" he mentions must be "worth doing." We can kill our countryside art with wised-up "audience-related" non-art, in which the producer promises he is starting "where the people are at." The people are, as they ever were, at the point of starvation for excellence. They want to do art themselves, and to share in the grand and ancient things. Not cynicism but humor will be needed.

# Enemy Evenings

In Minnesota towns one sometimes has the feeling of moving among ghosts, because we don't meet and talk to our local opponents on any question. We know, for example, that somewhere in our town of 2,242, there live people who believe that the preservatives sodium nitrite, sodium nitrate, and BHA variously threaten future health, and also in town live the local staff of the Agricultural Extension Division, who have just published an essay saying the advantages of these preservatives outweigh the disadvantages. Yet these two sets of people don't meet each other on open panels, and scarcely at all even privately, thus providing another major American issue which small-town people are left out of.

The case is always made that to keep a town from flying apart you must discuss only matters in which there is little conflict. That means that whenever a woman physician enters a room in which a few people are urging, intriguingly enough, that the man should be head of the woman (St. Paul), the topic must automatically be changed to whether or not we are getting that hard winter they kept talking about last fall.

There is nothing much wrong with weather talk except that far from preventing people from feeling "threatened" it is in fact the living proof that you don't care about those people: you haven't any interest in their thoughts; you don't want to hear them out.

There is little lonelier than small-town life when small talk is the principal means of peace. Sherwood Anderson illustrated it long ago, but people who still read Anderson seem to do so in a mist of nostalgia rather than for any revelation we can put to use. Also, I'm not content with the usual explanations for small-town citizens' being so uneasy around intense feelings. The question is: why are thousands and thousands of lively and feeling people who live in the countryside willing to give up, for their whole lives, the kind of friendship people enjoy who deliberately, curiously, and civilly draw out one another's views on serious subjects?

The reason generally offered, of course, is that airing last night's hassle at the church council will curtail this morning's sale of advertising space in the paper. This reason presupposes that serious exchange is a *hassle,* and must be the result of gaucherie. I don't believe it. Another commonly offered explanation is that less-informed or less-intelligent people will feel unequal to frank self-expression in the presence of more-informed or more-intelligent people. That is abundantly untrue. I have heard extremely strong opinions plentifully and bravely offered by people including myself who could hardly have been less informed or less gifted about the subject.

We simply need experience in taking an interest in the other side and doing so with the proponents of the other side present. If we could get this habit going I think we could reduce one of the most dismal characteristics of small-town life—the loneliness. Of course human loneliness is general, but this particular source of it, exercised in hypocrisy, could be ended.

Therefore, I propose that small community groups develop panels for Enemy Evenings. Obviously some much better word has to be used, but I like the pure madness of this one: it reminds me of that fantastic creation of Nixon, Ehrlichman, and Haldeman—the enemies list. Enemy Evenings would definitely need two things: a firm master of ceremonies in whom general affection for human beings would be paramount, not a chill manner or a childish desire to get the fur flying; second, it would need very just panel representation. An example of unjust panel representation would be a four-person panel to discuss the defense budget made up of a leader of American Writers vs. the Vietnam War; a director of Episcopal Community Services, Minneapolis; Senator Mondale; and (the chump) an American Party spokesman. It would be helpful too, if controversial panels were conducted with humor, but that isn't essential.

In discussing this notion at a Cultural Affairs Committee meeting in my town, we observed with interest the 1974–75 policy of the Minnesota Humanities Commission, emphasizing the relation between private concerns and public policies. Also, the National Endowment for the Humanities (through the Upper Midwest Council) has supported a series of television dialogues this winter, covering controversial subjects. All that is interesting, but for the common viewer what is seen on television is irrevocably "something they had on television." Seeing one's own neighbor speak out passionately (and having the chance to respond) is immediately engaging.

Here is a suggested rough list of seldom-discussed subjects with strongly opposed participants:

1. Additives in commercial food products and the relationship of 4-H instruction materials to the Wheat Institute.
   Suggested participants:
   > Home Extension personnel
   > Local members, the International Academy for Preventive Medicine
2. Fertilizing methods
   Suggested participants:
   > County agent
   > Anhydrous ammonia dealers
   > Bag fertilizer dealers
   > Soil Conservation Service Experiment station personnel

Members of the Soil Improvement Association

Local subscribers to Department of Natural Resources publications and *Organic Gardening,* and readers of U.S. Agricultural yearbooks

3. Fall plowing vs. spring plowing
    Suggested participants:

County agent (The official Ag. stand now is that fall plowing is detrimental, but by far the largest number of farmers still do it when they have time.)

Farmers committed to both plowing practices

4. Defense Department budget of the United States
    Suggested participants:

VFW or Legion Auxiliary officers

VFW or Legion Post officers

Local members, Women's League for Peace and Freedom

Local members, Common Cause

National Guard unit officers

5. St. Paul's stand on man as the head of woman
    Suggested participants:

Fundamentalist church representatives

Local Charismatic Christians—who tend to be nicely divided on this, providing an interesting confusion

Local members of Business and Professional Women's Clubs

Local Officers of American Federation of Women's Clubs

Grain elevator managers

6. The growth of shopping malls *around* small towns
    Suggested participants:

Local promoters of comprehensive plans

Main Street businessmen

Members of senior citizens' clubs

High school Ecology Club members

The mayor or council members

7. The emphasis on technical training at the high school level

Suggested participants:

Local painters, writers, and musicians

Vocational center director and staff

Visiting college humanities division members

Visiting Vo-Tech schools' faculty members

8. Drainage ditches

Suggested participants:

County commissioners and engineers holding contracts for ditches

Soil Improvement Association members

DNR staff members on loan

SCS personnel on loan

9. Competition vs. cooperation, as taught in U.S. elementary schools

Suggested participants:

Angry parents on both sides

School counselor

Fifth- or sixth-grade faculty members

Psychology faculty from neighboring community colleges

10. The lives of men and women in rural towns

Suggested participants:

President of the Jaycees

President of the Mrs. Jaycees

Larry Batson or Robert T. Smith of the *Minneapolis Tribune* or anyone half so lively

Very conservative pastors or priests

Personnel from West Central Mental Health Center

A painful fact of American life is that people from small towns are afraid of directness. Small-town kids, unlike suburban kids, can't take much from the shoulder. Example: A suburban Minneapolis child with a first-rate music instructor goes off to her piano lesson. She is working up a small piece of Mozart, she hasn't done her homework, and she smears the counting. The music instructor tells her it's an irresponsible job, sloppy phrasing, whatever she tells her—in any case, it won't do. The child returns home and works the piece up much more conscientiously next time, having learned that music is a disciplined pleasure.

A rural piano student cannot be spoken to so plainly. It is hard for her to be stirred into being responsible to the music at hand because the instant a teacher tries to correct her directly her soul sags into mere self-condemnation. Our style, in the countryside, is not to criticize children at all: we very seldom tell them the plane model was glued carelessly and the sleeve set in without enough easing. (The counterpart of this is that we seldom praise them much for anything either. "You played a real good game against Dawson"; "You did a real good job of that speech contest"—not "I knew you'd do well at the speech thing: I didn't know that I would cry—in fact, I'm *still* moved by what you said!") So the children develop neither stamina about criticism nor the imagination to picture to themselves gigantic praise if they excel. They live lightly handed into a middle world of little comment, and therefore little incitement to devotion. Should a music teacher try to explain Mozart's involvement in the music—what *he* had in mind for this or that phrase—the student wouldn't hear over the ground noise of dismay in her own feelings. "I'm being attacked! I'm being attacked!" is all her inexperienced soul can take in. Piranhas when you're out swimming, mean music teachers when you're taking piano—it's all the same to her. On a psychological ladder, she is rungs below being able to move from self to Mozart.

What we need in rural life is more Serious Occasion. By the time a child is ten, he or she should have heard, at least a few hundreds of times, "I loved that dying cowboy routine. Do it again. Do be quiet, Uncle Malcolm. Noah's going to do his dying cowboy routine." And adults would have shut up, listened, and praised. That moment would have been a Serious Occasion. Then a child is caught lying. It is horrible to lie—the notice of it should be serious and major. Then lying—whether or not one did it—is the subject of a Serious Occasion. Then, after some hundreds of such occasions, one can take in a conversation about music—what does Mozart want out of this piece? Remember: we are not now talking about you or yourself. We are talking about someone *other*—a musician long dead—and he is making a demand on us, and we are going to meet that demand! We are not going to scream and flee, because discipline is not the same thing as piranhas in the river.

I think we will surge into twice as much life through Serious Occasion.

At the same time, Minnesota rural life gives comfort and sweetness. Our young people are always returning home on their college weekends. When they drop out of college they tend to wander back here instead of prowling the streets of San Francisco or St. Paul. Apparently they garner genuine comfort from the old familiarity, the low-intensity social life, and with it a pretty good guarantee of not being challenged. Their ease has been bought, however, at the expense of the others who live here year round. To preserve our low-key manners, they have had to bottle up social indignation, psychological curiosity, and intellectual doubt. Their banter and their observations about the weather are carapace developed over decades of inconsequential talk.

The problem isn't like the major psychological phenomena in the United States—the increasing competitiveness and cheating in Ivy League and other top colleges, the multiplication of spies and counterspies in private corporations, the daily revelations of crookedness and irresponsibility on the part of major corporations, the ominous pursuance of the Law of the Sea conventions regardless of Cousteau's warnings, the overriding of public opinion about strip mining in the West. These are the horrible things that depress everybody. Remembering them, I think we can skip toward solving small-town dilemmas rather cheerfully. I commend frank panel evenings with opponents taking part: let's try that for a change of air, after years of chill and evasive tact.

# Great Snows

*How strange to think of giving up all ambition!*
*Suddenly I see with such clear eyes*
*The white flake of snow*
*That has just fallen in the horse's mane.*
                —"Watering the Horse," by Robert
                   Bly, *Silence in the Snowy Fields*

It is sometimes mistakenly thought by city people that grown-ups don't love snow. They think only children who haven't got to shovel it love snow, or only people like the von Fürsten-burgs and their friends who get to go skiing in exotic places and will never backslope a roadside in all their lives: that is a mistake. The fact is that most country or small-town Minneso-tans love snow. They relish snow in large inconvenient storms; they like the excesses of it, they like the threat of it, the endless work of it, the glamour of it.

Before a storm, Madison is full of people excitedly laying in food stocks for the three-day blow. People lay in rather celebra-tory food, too. Organic-food parents get chocolate for the chil-dren; weight watchers lay in macaroni and Sara Lee cakes; re-cently-converted vegetarians backslide to T-bones. People hang around the large Super-Valu window and keep a tough squinty-eyed watch on the storm progress with a lot of gruff, sensible observations (just like Houston Control talking to the moon, very much on top of it all) like "Ja, we need this for spring moisture . . ." or "Ja, it doesn't look like letting up at all . . ." or "Ja, you can see where it's beginning to drift up behind the VFW." The plain pleasure of it is scarcely hidden.

That is before the storm. Then the town empties out as the farmers and their families take their stocks home before U.S. 75, Minnesota 40, and Lac Qui Parle 19 close up. During the storm itself heroism is the routine attitude. I remember once when the phone was out, before all the telephone lines went underground, and the power was off, our neighbor came lightly in his huge pack boots across the drift top, high up from our house level, like an upright black ant, delicately choosing his footing over the hard-slung and paralyzed snow waves. He looked as if he were walking across a frozen North Atlantic. He had come over to see if we were O.K. It was before snowmobiles, at −40 degrees a welcome gesture.

Then right after a storm we all go back uptown because we have to see how the town has filled. The streets are walled ten and eleven feet high. If they had had underground parking ramps in the pyramids this is what they'd have looked like, white-painted, and we crawl between the neatly carved clean walls. The horrible snow buildup is a point of pride. In 1969 a fine thing happened: the county of Lac Qui Parle imported a couple of gigantic snow-removal machines from Yellowstone Park. It cost several thousand dollars to get those monsters here; when they arrived our heavy, many-layered, crusted snow broke the machines—they couldn't handle it. With glittering eyes we sent them back to Yellowstone Park.

Snowdrifts in the bad years, as in 1969, force us to dump garbage and nonburnables ever nearer the house, until finally in March there is a semicircle of refuse nearly at the front door. Even the German shepherd lowers his standards; the snow around the doghouse entrance is unspeakable.

If one has any kind of luck one garners comfort from great weather, but if there is some anxious and unresolved part of one's inner life, snowfall and certainly snowboundness can make it worse. During the winter of 1968–69, the three doctors of our town prescribed between two and three times as much tranquilizing medicine as usual. And Robert Frost, despite being one of the best snow poets going, has an odd, recurring fretfulness about snow:

> The woods are lovely, dark and deep,
> But I have promises to keep

What promises? To whom? If we think about it it sounds moralistic and self-denying—a moral showing-off in some way. The nervousness is stronger, though, in "Desert Places":

> Snow falling and night falling fast, oh, fast
> In a field I looked into going past,
> And the ground almost covered smooth in snow,
> But a few weeds and stubble showing last.
>
> The woods around it have it—it is theirs.
> All animals are smothered in their lairs.
> I am too absent-spirited to count;
> The loneliness includes me unawares.

I am struck by the malaise of the word *absent-spirited*. It must mean—this joy in snow or fretfulness in snow—that whatever is providential and coming to each of us from within is sped the faster by snowfall.

Being out in a blizzard is not lovely. Nature then feels worse than inimical; it feels simply impersonal. It isn't that, like some goddess in Homer, she wants to grab and freeze your body in her drifts; it is that you can be taken and still the wind will keep up its regular blizzard whine and nothing has made a difference. In February of 1969 the fuel men couldn't get through for weeks; one midnight my husband and I had to transfer oil from a drum behind an old shed to our house tank. We did this in cans, load after load, crawling on all fours and rolling in the ravines between the drifts. It had some nice moments: every ten minutes or so we'd meet behind the old shed, when one returned an empty can and the other was coming away with a full one, and we'd crouch in the scoured place, leaning over the nasty, rusted, infuriatingly slow spigot of the oil tank there. Looking at each other, we saw we had that impersonal aspect of snow-covered people. It was peculiar to think that anyone behind those freezing, melting, refreezing eyebrows ever objected to an act of Congress or ever loved a summer woods or memorized the tenor to anything by Christopher Tye. Back inside, our job done, still cold and rough-spoken, still walking like bears, we studied the children in their beds.

To us in Minnesota a blizzard in itself is of no practical good, but it is interesting how useful blizzards can be. Ordinary snowfall, not moved into deep-packed areas by wind, runs off too quickly in the spring and can't be controlled for good use. The *Proceedings of the American Society of Civil Engineers* has essay after essay on uses of Rocky Mountain snowmelt. Twenty-five hundred years ago, and possibly even earlier, the Persians used deep-drifted snow for irrigation. They built their *qanats*. Qanats are brick-walled tunnels running from the snowfields of the Elburz and other mountain ranges of Iran to villages fifteen or twenty miles away. At a point in the mountains' water table still higher than the land level of the parched miles and miles to be irrigated, the arched brick tunnels were carefully sloped to keep the water moving. The "mother well" was 200 feet deep and deeper. These 22,000 tunnels (there were 30,000 in 1960 but 8,000 were not in working condition) had airshafts for fresh air and maintenance access every 50 to 60 yards. Darius took the qanat technique to Egypt in the 5th century B.C. Nothing could have been cultivated in three-fourths of the now-irrigated fields of Iran without the ancient qanats. Persia was the originator of melons, cucumbers, and pears.

This is just to give an idea of mankind's long use of heavily drifted snow. Since we don't *use* blizzards in western Minnesota, the question lingers: why the pleasure in great weather? As with children in thunderstorms, I think we all have a secret affair of long standing with the other face of things. Children want the parents and the police and the other irritating powers to have their measure taken; they want a change of justice; but it goes further: they have a secret affection for bad weather.

Storms, what is more, force us to look at nature closely, and that is never boring. All meetings of the Business Improvement Association and the Countryside Council and the play rehearsal committees stop in a blizzard. It is a help. Two things make nature lovely to people, I think: enforced, extended leisure in a natural place—which storms give us out here; and second, planning our own lives instead of just following along. The moment, for example, that someone finally decides not to take the promising job offered by Reserve Mining, for example, or the moment someone decides not to pad a travel-expense account at the Ramada is a moment in which ice and snow and bare trunks look better, less happenstance, less pointless. C. S. Lewis goes very far: he claims that the fact that we all agree on what is meant by *good* or *holy* (that is, no one thinks robbery or despoiling the land or depriving the poor is good) indicates that goodness and holiness are actually a normal, planned part of our universe—perfectly natural to the species. He would not be surprised at all to see snow on a horse's mane all the better for having just worked out an ethical decision.

# Extended vs.
# Nuclear Families

I have been thinking about the positive side of a Minnesota blizzard. Another of the blessings is that extended-family occasions come to a halt. Thank goodness. The extended-family dinner is a threat to the pleasure and ease of the American farm family, yet it is hard to say so. In Minnesota we are great protectors of the American family—just as we are one of the last areas in which the small "family farm" idea works and is sacred. We are right about this. The nuclear family is far the best of all the units human beings organize themselves into; when you break it down, its members inevitably pursue lesser, not greater, aims. They settle for cheaper values. Jung says that, when the family breaks, the adult members tend to be frozen at the level of consciousness at the moment of the break. On a less subtle level, people begin following their own noses with more abandon. Experiment takes the place of solid satisfaction; satisfaction takes the place of thinking hard.

In the country, *family* means father, mother, children, and the grandparents; *extended family* would mean all the above plus the cousins, the uncles, the grownup in-laws on a lot of sides. These relations tend still to be living near one another, and often a farm couple's first five or six Christmases together will be spent in their presence.

The extended-family goals are not the nuclear-family goals; what nourishes extended-family society is starvation fare for the nuclear family. Here is how it works. If people are eccentric and verbal and curious about other lifestyles, then the extended-family dinner plus afternoon plus supper plus afterward is a cheerful, messy, engaging, affectionate business even when it does drag on all day (as it always does). But if people are shy or harassed or not perfectly confident about their accomplishments, then the extended-family holiday is informed by some misery along with the Jell-O and fruit and Rice Crispie bars.

My suspicion is that prairie families have been ruing these large, hearty, 100 percent threatening occasions for over a century now, but no one dares say anything because it sounds mean—and it does sound awfully mean to say you don't want the whole family back over this year. If you took a poll with promise of utter secrecy I feel sure the vote would be 98 percent: We Should Have Gathered only two times instead of four times this year because I was never so tense or bored in my life, and 2 percent: Well, Merv and LaVonne had them last year, so we figured it was up to us to have them all this year. Such remarks never get made aloud, however, because our general cultural stance in the countryside is that we wish people "neighbored" more, the way they used to, and we wish families were sticking together more, the way they used to. Who can imagine Laura Ingalls Wilder wishing the folks were not all going to show up? In other words, we are torn about this.

I will describe what works badly in big family occasions. Unlike lions and dogs, we are a dissenting animal. We need to dissent in the same way that we need to travel, to make money, to keep a record of our time on earth and in dream, and to leave a permanent mark. Dissension is a drive, like those drives. Our greatest thinkers, the only ones that do us much good, are the dissenters. (It is the toneless lemmings who keep proffering "sharing" and "affirmation.") Orwell and Tolstoy and Jesus and Rachel Carson and Socrates don't suggest we "share" or "affirm" values. They all beg us to use the part of us that dissents. It is the part that shouts "This is frightful! I want to think about it! I want the frightfulness to sift, leisurely, through me, so I've got the feel of it! Then—and not until then—I'll try to act!"

For that kind of thinking and feeling we need gravity. We need a chance to be slow, turbid, and grave. Nothing could be worse for this than to be desperately busy all week, week in, week out, at hard physical work and then have a whole valuable, holy holiday taken up by an extended-family occasion. There is little chance to talk about anything. If one says, "Well, the Farmers Union has an interesting project on hand—they're bringing the humanities to nontraditional audiences," a responsible hostess is likely to respond: "Oh—if you're going to talk politics then . . . " And if one says, "You know, I often wonder what happens in that bourn from which no traveller returns—you know? I mean, what dreams'll come when we've shuffled off etc?" a responsible hostess might say, "Oh, for morbid . . . " I don't know why it is that in large family gatherings it is morbid to discuss life after death, whereas it is good, workable smalltalk to discuss accidents involving young fathers and bailing-wire winders on their tractors, or the mutilation of cattle by some occult group.

Lions are a more suitable animal for extended-family gatherings than country people. Their time isn't valuable, for one thing. No animal spends less of its time gathering food or contriving shelter than the African lion; no animal spends more of its time in prides (extended-family excursions), flat on its back napping, paws sticking up.

The traditional weapon against time wasting by the extended family was the nineteenth- and twentieth-century prep, or public, school. School was valued as a higher loyalty than the family. Honoring family was a given; a sign of growing up was to have a school to honor. Country was to follow. The loyalty that would have made the young person sit around and nod politely throughout Thanksgiving, Christmas, and New Year's Day, to the cheer of Aunt LaVonne and Uncle Merv, went instead to the school, or to the Army. At its worst, this evolved loyalty went to the school tie and ended there. At its best, I suppose, it went to the eternal communion of writers and their audiences—to whoever made us shout at first reading of him or her, "That's it!" School or army are assumed to be higher loyalties; it is acceptable to rise from a foundering dinner of turkey with "Sorry, people, but I've an exam to study for! Wish I hadn't!" or "Sorry, people, I have to pack, I'm supposed to be at Fort Bragg tomorrow!" whereas it doesn't work the other way round: no one writes Headmaster Sizer that they'll be back at Andover a few days late because Merv and LaVonne and their kids are here from Colorado Springs. And apparently guardhouses and brigs are kept in business by people who try on such explanations in the armed services.

A drawback to Midwest rural life has been our serious need to "neighbor," which has locked us into rather more of the extended-family social life than is good for us. We feel torn about this: there was something great in the coming and going of neighbors from pioneer times right up to World War II. Yet it is a terrific relief not to have these invasions—which tend to last for hours. And so we have developed some minor, peripheral social occasions which very few city people could guess at. On Sunday mornings, a couple of men spend an hour parked in one of their snow-cleared farmyards. A farmer drives his heated pickup over to the neighbor's farmyard, and waits for his friend to out and join him in the cab. They sit there for a while, warmed by the heater, listening to the calm engine. They don't want the house; the house is given over to the conventional things—preparation of Sunday dinner, going to Sunday school. They sit with some beer in the pickup. It is very important, because they are outside convention and also free of work. Another place like that, at another season, is the unused stall of the 4-H buildings at the county fair. Somehow people have found a few straw bales left, and skewed them around into a circle, and they can really talk. In the next stall the heavy Hereford stands; just looking at him you can tell it isn't enough to be *of nature*. We were meant to work out ideas. The city person who retires to country life hasn't the problem of the regular country resident: his situation is free of extended family. No one expects him to show up for New Year's Day dinner and then stay all the afternoon and then eat leftover turkey.

There are conversations that can kill:

"Ja, you can sure tell there's more snow coming from where that came from."

or

"You're a lot safer in a jet than you are on U.S. 212 I don't care what they say."

The problem with the above remarks is not that they're untrue or dull: it is that one can't reply, "To tell you the truth, I think I'm on the other side of that one." It is impossible to dissent.

Why all the fuss about dissenting? Educators, beginning with Piaget, I think, tell us firmly that the mind literally is *changed*, evolved, by the act of conceiving a new idea. It's no longer the same mind. We all need to have this experience; so apparently we need hours and hours of conceptualizing. We have finally got it through our heads, too, that what one class of people needs, all the classes of people have a right to. It isn't just Beethoven who needs silence and gravity: it's all of us. And that means, especially for most of us who are madly moonlighting to make enough money, that it is cruel to waste our precious winter holidays with structured family gatherings.

The true good of blizzards is that Mervin and LaVonne get

to stay in Colorado Springs and we get to stay at home without them. The schoolbus can't get through, so the children are home. No one can get out to work, so the adults are home. There is no conventional structure for nuclear-family-behavior-during-blizzards, so we face one another with delight and surprise. Anything gets said. The closeness, as the wind screams around the light pole and builds up its incredible drifts, which later we will tunnel, is absolutely lovely. If whoever of us, like Hamlet, should now wonder aloud how it is without the mortal coil, no one need kill that with "Oh, for morbid!" because the house is full of confidence. Dozens of times I've heard farm men and women mention how cozy it was during the storm—"We did whatever we liked; we talked a lot."

Most people have to worry about money most of the time, and then the relations dictate the holiday agenda. There is a lot of conscience in rural Minnesota, too. We stick by the cousins and uncles. So it is wonderful when the blizzards come and set us into an extraordinary situation.

Puritans need the extraordinary situation.

# Quietly Thinking Over Things at Christmas

The winter solstice is the ancient season of joining spirit and animal. In the old dances, people dressed as animals, the Morris men holding deer's heads before their faces and carrying a hobbyhorse for the Abbots Bromley horn dance; and a wren was hunted and killed, to make way for the new king. Swedish children, in fact, still think of Staffan (St. Stephen) as the patron saint of horses; in their archaic, beautiful carol *"Staffan var en stålledrang!"* St. Stephen has two red ponies, two white ponies, and one dappled. He is set upon and murdered in the forest, and his body arrives home on horseback. We don't celebrate Christ's resurrection at Christmas because that is the *parting* of body and spirit; we celebrate His birth, the *joining* of body and spirit. It is a terrific season in Minnesota: children left free to grow inward are remarkably dreamy from late October through Twelfth Night to the dullness of late January.

Then how doubly cruel that our Midwest society operates to deprive huge segments of the populace of quiet thinking for themselves, especially at Christmastime. Thousands are brought up to be respectful of this or that sacred subject—family life, church activity, Christmastime, motherhood, the office of the American presidency. Any sacred cow is a curse in that it must be taken as a whole—its core, its history, and its aura, all in one. It is taboo to separate sacred subjects into their parts and say, this two-thirds is okay, this one-third is rot. Whenever a *whole* subject is sacred, we cannot think about it quietly. And, if we are not allowed quiet thought, the lie somewhere in the subject begins to grow inside us, and we feel the lie and become frenetic in our efforts to suppress it, and then we become distrustful of other people because they might wake up the part that is lie. We become addicted to not "rocking the boat."

When we think about it, we notice that rocking the boat—the greatest anathema in small-town life—consists nearly entirely of dividing a subject into its components and treating the several components differently one from the other. For example, when people in Madison began speaking of Nixon's crookedness, several of our town leaders remarked that they wished "they'd just drop the whole Watergate thing" before the United States was "blown wide open." I thought that was very interesting, because it meant that Nixon could not be taken as one component of the nation; the society, the presidency, the national polity and psyche, all apparently were felt to be welded together and would either survive or be "blown wide open" together. Yet we know the reverse is true: when you take a rotten potato out of the barrel, in good time, you save the barrel, you don't "blow it wide open." In other words, there is a sanity in treating parts of anything separately.

It is considered rocking the boat to say that the Lutheran Church is a drag, although we all know it is a drag; yet it is very likely that if the hypocritical and heartless elements of church life were brought out into the open, like Watergate, truth and some new strength for reform might well race in and fill the spaces.

It is rocking the boat to find that a city council has floated a crooked bond issue on a building, for example; yet we all know that every time such corruption is exposed it has helped, not destroyed, the town. The businessmen who remained honest throughout are brought closer together.

Or to take a small instance: it is rocking the boat to read Eliot's "Journey of the Magi" at Christmas to a rural study club because Christmas is a "joyous family season" and Eliot is frank, full of solitude, and "very different." He reminds us of a part of Christmas that is like death, and that Christmas presages death. Here is a poem of Auden's which is quiet and thoughtful; it doesn't break new ground—its strength is in its taking up *part* of Christmas instead of trying, frenetically, to be enthusiastic about the whole:

> There are enough
> Left-overs to do, warmed-up, for the rest of the week—
> Not that we have much appetite, having drunk such a lot,
> Stayed up so late, attempted—quite unsuccessfully—
> To love all our relatives, and in general
> Grossly overestimated our powers. Once again
> As in previous years we have seen the actual Vision and failed
> To do more than entertain it as an agreeable
> Possibility, once again we have sent Him away
> Begging though to remain His disobedient servant,
> The promising child who cannot keep His word for long.

This is quiet, and absorbing, in comparison to the frantic uplift and clean bounce of *Christmas Ideals* magazine. It is cruel to condition people against reading such poems as Eliot's or Auden's.

Inexperience with quiet thought has another side effect in Minnesota: a residual, rather habitual chill between men and women. This is the way it seems to work. Nearly all of us women feel it our job to keep up civilization; we have an ancient conviction that if we don't keep it up the men will ease backward through evolution, with their socks and their hauteur, the way Poland Chinas turn back into wild boars with such frightening speed. So if we believe that Christmas's character as a "joyous season" and "a family time" is a civilizing notion, we feel constrained to uphold it. A part of us says Yes, but why are we frenetic and miserable at Christmas then? and why is the suicide rate so high at Christmas?

The answer must be in the components of Christmas—two-thirds may be joyous family material, but at least one-third must be introversion and contemplation and animal celebration: julebokking* isn't an accident! We "horse around" during the days of Christmas; it is the season of horses and mischief. But Midwest housewives aren't free to do mischief! Or to consider this sacred subject in its components. So they are stuck, still sitting cold in church circle meetings saying, "Christmas is a joyous family time," feeling the partial lie of it. Meanwhile, the husband also suffers from the lie. Because he is likely not to be so conditioned to passivity as his wife, he fights the lie. He goes down to the VFW lounge or somewhere, somewhere dark and damned and against the pious tone of the town, and the hell with it: he is going to do some serious drinking; that is, he is going to recover, somehow, feelings he has repressed.

I've seen a certain expression in men's faces in places like VFW lounges, but only recently have I understood this look: it is a look of deliberate *intelligence*. You have all the rest as well, of course—the boorish leaning over the carelessly mixed drinks, the beastly canned music, the spasmodic, loud, halting conversations, which some idiot at intervals contrives to liven up with a joke by which Norway, Poland, or Israel is the loser—there is all that, of course—but there is a very common expression of true cunning and a will to see straight: the men's eyes stare and look bald. I now understand that look to mean that they have come to recover suppressed knowledge which their wives or their town won't let them uncover elsewhere, not for a moment. They have come to say the damned things: all our leaders in Washington are a bunch of bad-language nouns, and big businessmen who have control of everything have bad-language verbed the country, and this being conned

---

*Julebokking—Christmas joking, the Norwegian equivalent of the horsing around with fools' masses, etc.

into buying presents is a lot of collective bad-language noun, and in family life—in raising kids—a human being is somehow partially bad-language past participled by raising a family at all. All this is an attempt to recognize the bad fraction of sacred wholes.

If the men could succeed in recognizing that, they would win for themselves the old joy of *quietly thinking about things.* What happens, however, is that the man returns home, excited by the shadow material that has been seen and said—he drives home really excited. The sodium-lighted main street and the crescent-shaped pile of plowed snow around a car that wasn't moved off before the plow came by and the gritted railroad tracks at the level crossing—all this feels like his own country and he is intact, in a glittering, frantic way. It is what is called having had a pretty good drunk. Then he arrives home and his wife, whether she spent the evening with him or waited at home, is snapped into her civilization-upholding stance. A drunk, idol-smashing man is a threat to civilization: he will uncover the one-third sacred subject she tries to suppress under family cheer; he will force her into *thought* instead of *reverence.* In a word, she is terrified. She snaps at him. And he is so vulnerable because his spirit is freed and has climbed outward nearly to his skin—in fact, it is nearly on his surface. He wants to go on considering truths here, truths there, he wants to give just desserts to this evildoer and that evildoer, and he wants to remark that such-and-such a wretched failure around town really has a good side to him, by God! He wants to consider things in their components. So, when his wife snaps at him in her pain, she attacks part of his spiritual life.

She has no idea what a stunning blow it is. All his quiet judgments leak back down through the great crack in him, before they ever had a chance to become genuine, quiet, thought-out and talked-about judgments; it has all poured down back through the crack as water drops with lightning speed into a fissure in the earth, vanishing, and then the crack itself closes, and he is locked out of his soul again for a while. A dull anger lies over the earth of him now, like a dust cloud above all these movings; as he and his wife glide around the living room, putting out lights near the nonflammable tree, the dull anger in him paws over toward her. Either everything is sacred (the point she stuck at) or everything is a big bunk (the point he had arrived at) and they don't evolve beyond that with each other.

If we are producing this scene over and over in our countryside we have a very mean side to our society. Perhaps we can work up a community of cures for that part of Minnesota life which isn't so lovely; I want to make two suggestions here. First, let us start teaching that women need not be positive about sacred occasions; they may be thinkers and pessimists. Second, let us start teaching that whenever something new or something old is to be discussed it should be discussed in its parts, severally. Not, then: How did you like the concert? but, Which part of the concert did you like least? which most? This will increase the accuracy of people's remarks. A trendy question that is going around in Minnesota now is the identity issue that hit the East Coast in the late 1950s: "Who am I? My God, I've got to have a clear sense of who I am!" It is astonishing that people should expect to identify the whole *I*, to come up with one answer. Any answer given to such a question is bound to contain a lie in it which will ferment anxiety, just as we see the anxiety in individual men and women suffering from sacred-cowism. Nearly any answer ought to be, I think: it is one-third this way, one-third that way, and there is a third I don't understand yet.

There is a casual relaxation in not pronouncing on whole subjects. If the women of the Midwest could learn to be casual instead of pious, they could drop those defenses; they could entertain one-third pessimism on countless subjects, which would make possible thoughtful conversation with each other and men. They could release themselves and men from lip service

to family life and motherhood and the holiness of being together all the time: they could stop *upholding* this value and
that value and just comment together. Then the men, in turn,
could use their own homes instead of the VFW lounge to ex-
plore unconscious material. I think it would help tremendously, because when you go to the VFW-lounge sort of place you
tend to turn *all* to bunk—which is only the flip side of holding
*all* sacred. The end result of that syndrome is the Dean Martin
show, in which every single decent thing there is, from animal
life to the United States Senate, even the private life of Senator
Humphrey, is compulsively attacked with the intent of reduc-
ing it to trash. That is self-hatred, not quiet thought.

Viewing things in their component parts makes reform possible, too. If "the whole country's going to the dogs" you can't
reform anything, but if one-third of the country is going to the
dogs, you can decide precisely *which* third (or other fraction)
and work to get it out. We can't fire the whole CIA; we could
work at eliminating all those who conspired to ruin Allende,
for example.

It is interesting that the Southern white woman is conditioned, much as is the Midwestern woman, to be cheerful and extroverted, and to honor sacred cows while a young woman. But
then there comes a significant difference: In middle age the
Southerner is expected to change roles: she becomes an accurate commenter on human nature, rich in earthy metaphor
even, the one who cuts through falseness—even a *femme horrible*. It must be a terrific relief! And there is a playfulness to it,
which no one can say the Lutheran Church encourages here.
Our women, and men often, are stuck upholding sacred cows
until their fifties and sixties. I have been working with senior
citizens recently, and I have noticed with interest and surprise
that at seventy and seventy-five Midwestern women who have
been conventional do finally get free of positive thinking and
upholding institutions, and they can become the most marvelous sharers of this or that tough truth—and they gain the sin-

gular playfulness that goes with not lying to oneself any more.

When a frank and quiet person like that *does* praise something finally, it isn't the perfunctory flagwaving kind of thing at all; when a free person comments on Christ's being made man at Christmas, for example, the effect is not the frantic theology of habitual liars.

# To Unteach Greed

For the moment, at least, we are stuck with advising high schoolers that they must expect to take jobs they don't look forward to, because the interesting ones are too rare. In my hometown, for example, six or seven of each high school class express an interest in forestry, parks, and similar outdoor work, but the vocational school that trains for those jobs, Brainerd, has only thirteen openings a year. Girls want to be dental assistants, but St. Cloud, which has the appropriate program, gets three hundred applications for its forty places. Minnesota city dwellers may find it odd but it is nonetheless true that to get into farming—and I use the term here to mean just to get a job as a hand—you have to "know somebody." The good jobs, which by their nature are satisfying to sense and sensibility, are cruelly hard to land.

Therefore, a realistic high school counselor teaches kids to get ready for disappointment. He or she may seem a villain in steering young people to the 600,000 clerk-typist openings when they want forestry, or in not making a whole lot out of the Phillips (Andover, Massachusetts) Academy's imaginative Short Term Institutes—six weeks' programs for high school kids from around the country, designed to give them the idea of knowledge-for-the-joy-of-it before they get washed into the

Vo-Tech stream of cost/benefit thinking. It seems tough to advise kids that someone must work in the deafening assembly lines; why not advise them someone must staff the top offices everywhere, and raise their expectations to that?

The counselors are being realistic, and their advice isn't cruel. What *is* cruel is that we do not teach a decent philosophical way to look at life; so that those in our countryside who work with hands or head are misled, and waste years finding their inner life. People are taught to be drones.

Only once in a public information meeting in my part of the country have I heard the farm populace approached as if they were people with anything but money making in their heads. In countless Countryside Council meetings, countless Democratic party meetings, countless senior citizens' group meetings (which I went to when working on a minibus task force) and nearly always in Lutheran Church meetings—where the ministers are constantly saying, "We think too much of money," as if money consciousness were a uniform, requisite sin—in all these public meetings the audience was regarded as people wanting profit or high income only. The schools assume that even the children will be interested only in profit and high income. Once I saw a sixth-grade movie against shoplifting in which the two motives provided for not shoplifting were

1. you might be caught, and if you have a police record it will be hard to get a job;
2. shoplifting indirectly raises prices so you eventually will have to pay more for things;

both reasons being self-interest. Nowhere did the movie say,

1. it is mean to shoplift;
2. you do not want to be an unkind person.

The single occasion on which I heard an adult group out here addressed as if they had any moral nature or philosophical nature at all was April 2, 1977, at a 208 Water Quality meeting arranged by the 6-W Regional Development Commission. The speaker, Judge Miles Lord, said, "You farmers can act on motivations beyond greed . . . you can think of natural resources in terms of sharing what we all have, not just in terms of exploitation."

It was rather a surprising address. One farmer, a panelist, was querulous because a Minnesota law made it illegal for us to dye our potatoes with that poisonous red dye but Missouri farmers could still dye theirs, so it was hard for a Minnesota potato producer and shipper to compete with the Missouri people (housewives still being ignorant enough of the chemical danger to buy potatoes because of the handsome color). The speaker's reply to this was "There speaks the voice of greed!" The audience was a little surprised. It was refreshing to hear the word aloud—*greed*—and to be expected to do better.

How refreshing it is to get to think about the moral aspect of things! How immensely boring our countryside life in Minnesota is, despite its beauty, for the simple reason we never get to consider the morals of things—together, publicly.

I have a practical suggestion to make to raise the moral consciousness out here. I suggest we keep or make English required of our juniors and seniors but with the following two strict conditions:

1. That *no techniques* of literature be taught or discussed ever. All approaches to stories being read must be to what they show of life—inner life, feelings, public life, morals.
2. And that we teach courses with a rural-literature emphasis.

Technique is the enemy of philosophy and goodness. The "technique or form creates content" attitude of the 1940s New Criticism makes for cold treatment of stories, deliberate mental superiority over literature—as if literature were something to be seen through. You see it in the frosty way English departments of universities and colleges, still stuck with that interest in technique, handle their freshman curricula. Tolstoy has a terrific passage in *Anna Karenina* against technique. Some art "appreciators" are in a painter's studio, looking at a picture he has just passionately finished in which Christ is one of the figures.

> "Yes—there's a wonderful mastery!" said Vronsky.... "There you have technique." ... The sentence about technique had sent a pang through Mihailov's [the painter's] heart, and looking angrily at Vronsky he suddenly scowled. He had often heard this word technique, and was utterly unable to understand ... a mechanical facility for painting or drawing, entirely apart from its subject.

Here is a tentative format for an Ag Lit course:

> *Akenfield*, especially the chapters about Muck Hill Farm and the Young Farmers' League, and the one about the old Scot who couldn't adjust to the new gardening ways
>
> "How Much Land Does a Man Need?" from Tolstoy's *Russian Stones and Legends*
>
> *Growing Up in Minnesota*, especially Robert Bly's strange chapter about the sheriff railroading a farmhand to jail in Madison, Minnesota
>
> *All Things Bright and Beautiful* and *All Creatures Great and Small*
>
> "To a Mouse" by Burns
>
> "Home Burial" and "The Hill Wife" by Frost
>
> *Furrow's End*, edited by D. B. Greenberg, especially the story of the young sheepherder and his girl from squatter background—one of the most terrific young-love stories with a farming scene
>
> *Winesburg, Ohio*
>
> *My Antonia*
>
> *String Too Short to Be Saved*, Donald Hall's autobiography, with a terrific chapter on a hired hand whose sole passion in life was Mounds bars.

These stories and poems should be read by people who are going to live in Minnesota small towns and on farms if they're lucky; and if the stories and verse are studied in the spirit in which they were written, instead of in the spirit of methodology, the young people may come to like English, and enjoy seeing what people think about life.

We especially need to do this if we can't have the jobs we want. If the competitive profit-making part of our lives is going to fall short, and it will for most, then the reflective, intuitive part of life had better be more rewarding than it is. A very nice by-product of an Ag Lit course would be something for men and women to talk about besides Starsky and Hutch. We need a thousand more things to ruminate about together out here. We need conversations that take in the moral aspect of things as well as their money-making aspect. It will bring to the country-side a sorely needed gentleness.

# Rural Feelings:
# Starting in the Mailroom
# and Having to Stay There

In one of the towns in my county, when the boys have lost an "away" game of football, they are not allowed to talk to each other in the bus coming home. The coach has made it clear to them they are supposed "to feel so bad about what they did, losing, that they shouldn't *want* to talk anyway."

I'd like to put another sports example next to that one: it used to be that when a boy on either team, home or visitors, was hurt on the field, the entire audience stood up and clapped quietly all the while he was being carried off. Now, however, at least in rural Minnesota, injuries to opponents are frequently greeted with "All *right!* All *right!*" Also, perhaps less infuriating, when an opponent in basketball misses his or her foul shot, there are cries of "All *right!* All *right!*" Filthy words still incur a technical foul, but the tawdriest lack of sportsmanship is, as in the case of the football team's ride home in silence, enforced, and, in the case of audiences shouting, "All *right!*," condoned.

During the 1950s when everyone still expected "to get ahead with the firm," *The New Yorker* ran a cartoon in which the company president was saying to someone from personnel: "Look, find me a man who will start in the mailroom and then stay there." The shadow side of Horatio Alger! Our Minnesota countryside is the mailroom of emotional life; people living in it are asked to settle for the least ennobling makeup of social relations, and then never to shake them off. In attitudes to community and country, two of the least ennobling feelings are (1) I and mine must win, the other must lose, and what's more, everything is a win-lose situation; and (2) everything is either ego-threatening or ego-supporting. Detachment does not exist. I must vigilantly ask, Does this threaten me or support me? Anyone can imagine what this does to conversation, political discussion, prayers in church, and visiting with American Field Service foreign students.

I used to accept the prevalent sociological assumption that the nervous ego-centered attitudes in the countryside arose from people feeling too uneducated to make judgments about anything beyond a firm prejudice about Kerr vs. Ball canning tops, "green stuff" (John Deere) vs. "red stuff" (International) in tractors, whether you get germs from taking communion from a chalice or not. Now I know the theory is wrong, and there is an ugly second source of this insecurity. We can get rid of it.

During the Middle Ages the Roman Catholic Church found that you could keep villagers from making trouble if their parish priests were from the same background. That is, you sent the country boy to Tours or Grenoble, then you quickly sent him back to his own or a similar village as a priest, with the understanding that he'd now got power over the others, and it was delicious power because the underlings were his own people.

No Alsatian takes much pleasure in holding down a white kitten under its great paw, but it is very pleased to get control over another Alsatian; if you watch carefully, whenever the dog that is being controlled moves slightly, the winner dog makes a parallel movement with his head and gives a warning growl that is very enlightening to the loser dog. In the Dark Ages there had been a lot of gentle-born parish priests—some of them later made saints—whose joy in examining their own spirit had caught on, and the peasant had begun to experience a thing called freedom of feeling.

It was not in the interests of the Church, however, that the intelligentsia and the peasantry should be joined in religious expression. The Church was then linking itself with feudal lords and, in its organizational style, imitating the Roman Empire. What was needed, from the churchman's point of view, then, was a local parish priest who would keep the peasantry in line. The best way to keep people in line is (a) to remove their access to intellectuals and (b) to set a few of their own peers just slightly over them, thus preserving a dismaying, endless power struggle in the villages. Callow or ill-qualified clerics kept the Christians nettled much of the time.

As time wore on, no one who lived his whole life in a village ever heard a fresh or impassioned thought. The only urgings one heard were toward piety and obedience. It was an early practice of behavior modification, and it worked. The Church won the power battle. Religious feelings got vague in the absence of true-minded teachers and, finally, independent spirit virtually vanished. Isolating the majority from expressive leaders is not a new idea: it is classic because it works. Pharaoh's Jews suffered it in Egypt, just as the Soviet Union has largely removed or isolated the independent intellectuals in all of the Iron Curtain countries.

We staff our small-town schools, logically, with people from other small towns in Minnesota. They are attuned to the life. But this isolates the children from people with a more relaxed attitude toward competition. The children, generally, are taught:

Praise the United States, never other countries.

Praise one's own town, never other towns.

Do not respond openly to others' activities: be passive in church and theatre, and clap only slightly at concerts.

Argue and win—do not simply converse.

Even our Family Life course for adults includes such instructions as "Recognizing the Children's Tricks and Dealing with Them." This means the mother is trained like a young lieutenant to forestall likely enemy moves. Anyone can imagine the lack of kindly ease this injects into the family.

To bring in another tone, I would like to suggest that experienced teachers in Minneapolis and St. Paul volunteer to exchange a year or two with teachers in rural (not suburban but really rural) high schools and grade schools. The Minnesota Humanities Commission might consider this quite logically within their purview of private concern and public authority. ESA (Education Service Association) and other groups could help with the salary differential. It would be interesting for us in Madison or Dawson or Appleton, for example, to have a retired or nearly-retired Breck School faculty member come out here, and teach "Heart of Darkness" as a study of people psychologically dumping on others. It would be interesting for our seniors to get a lesson on the Holy Grail as a theory of failing to find the inner life—how very long Gawain was getting the idea, but how worthwhile it all was. Meanwhile, one of our teachers could offer Blake or Shattuck a course in nineteenth-century farmers' politics in North Dakota considered in the light of U.S. railroad history and antitrust legislation. Or a team of one Madison English teacher and one Madison speech teacher could offer a Twin Cities school a senior course called "The American Heart—in Agriculture and in Literature," for which authors to read would include Ole Rölvaag, Stephen Vincent Benét, and Wendell Berry.

*Particulars* about American business can be discussed in peace; American business *as a whole* never can. We need teachers from the Twin Cities not only to exchange course offerings with us, but to join our civic groups for a year in order to share these specific, parts-of-wholes kinds of facts that we simply haven't got enough of here. We need to learn that balance of parts; we need to learn that Honeywell has made weaponry, but Honeywell supports the arts; we need to feel that what Honeywell does is no reflection on us; we will survive the discussion (as will Honeywell); there is nothing we must defend lest we be torn to bits. The whole idea of any truth as a detached value would bring in a huge cool wind of vitality. But, as Jung says, you can't really do much without a teacher at some point. I am asking for teachers of detachment to teach detachment in schools and in adult groups in our countryside.

We will know when we have left the mailroom of social life. On the bus home the coach will say, "Well, that was one super-extra-lousy game of football we played, except I'd like to say that such-and-such went well, and so-and-so was good hanging in there, and did you guys notice how their quarterback has gotten a lot better? Who else do we have to watch?"

Then the boys will have some sort of exhausted conversation, which like all restorative conversations, will begin grumpily and then, as you view the experience in a more and more detached way, will get almost cordial.

This will not wreck the marvelous male verve which wants to beat the dickens out of an opposing team. It will divide life from a whole, a whole made up of ego-nervousness, into two halves—the same old half of ego-nervousness in which you might get licked or you have to lick someone else, and the new, second half in which you yourself relax and nearly disappear, and you see other things, other people more clearly. Later, further divisions can be added, but in rural Minnesota we need to make this first one now.

# Even Paranoids Have Enemies!*

Most people in rural Minnesota seem to face evil seldom, inaccurately, and slothfully. It must be a general property of mankind to avoid dealing with actual evils as they show up; I'd like to describe how we do it in southwestern Minnesota.

Lutheran virtue is cheerful virtue, and since Lutheran virtue is strong in our towns and countryside, we are pressed to be pretty cheerful most of the time. It isn't cheerful to think of specific social evils, so our usual procedure is to point to the fantasy enemy *"they."*

*They* are familiar to us all, so, only briefly, here is what *they* do. They don't build cars or anything else the way they used to; they don't do an honest day's work any more; they don't care about the little guy; they are ruining the soil, the countryside, the American family, and the American family farm—and just about everything else. They, like the Devil, are legion, whereas *we* are singular, embattled, and helpless against them. They are *they*—plural: politically astute, cunning, and impersonal; we

* Attributed to Delmore Schwartz.

tend to be, psychologically, singular: the farmer, clean-cut, and minding our own business.

One reason we are minding our own business is that it's easier than taking part in government. We vaguely feel we ought to be taking part in government, though, so the rationalization is to create such a huger-than-life enemy—a kind of a pretend enemy rather than a real one, an enemy made up of contradictory parts—that we needn't fight him: it is hopeless. Here are the convenient aspects of the enemy *they:*

*They* are not the United States or any specific corporation or agency; therefore, our country and "the big shots" are kept on as father figures.

*They* do not reply when we complain. As Washington people constantly explain: we don't care how much you protest or what you protest as long as you name no names. So there is no danger of reprisal if we are not specific.

*They* include not just outer, real enemies—vague figures that resemble U.S. agencies or certain elements of the private sector—but also clumsy, smeary figures, somehow felt, hardly seen, inside our own unconscious. By cursing or accusing *them*, we attack anew our old mean parents or scary childhood figures: we get in a lick, so to speak, albeit late, against ghosts who did us wrong.

Midwest rural paranoia is heartfelt. We can't be deceived about that. Ridiculous as its symptoms sometimes are, it is a real psychic problem, involving real, submerged suffering, and resulting in stupid ways of life. The first noticeable thing about paranoia is the inaccuracy of its shafts. The following anecdote contains several of its elements:

In about 1957 a couple visited my husband and me, and we scarcely could bear the desultory conversation. All four of us were suffering. (I remember afterward my husband remarked that the boredom was so exquisite that tears came to his eyes several times during the afternoon.) At one point, however, the man suddenly announced: Well, the reason you can't count on the weather any more like you used to could is that all these jet airplanes flying over are wrecking it for the farmer.

All four of us perked up a little; paranoid fantasies have a kind of energy, in any case. We asked: Which jet flights? Northwest Airlines? North Central? Continental Defense Command from Duluth—or Strategic Air Command practice flights up from Wichita? Or what?

Instantly, both man and wife answered: "Oh no! None of them!"

I was interested in that sureness as to which were *not* the causes of the bad weather; they insisted on preserving a vague, unidentified enemy. They insisted on a *vague* sort of dread; an enemy in the sky, as opposed to near and walking like us—and (this is what indicates the presence of unconscious material in that enemy) an enemy that brought about the end of a Golden Age. In this case, the Golden Age is entirely phantasmal; it is when you used to be able to count on the weather—this concept despite the plagues of all the ages and the droughts of the 1930s and hail of the 1940s. The quick denial that those flights could originate with an airline with a name or an Air Force unit with a base shows, I think, that the couple in some part of their psyche *meant* to keep the enemy unreal, a pretend enemy, half conscious, who would receive their paranoid flailings.

Apart from attending a few special-interest meetings, most of us in rural Minnesota do not participate in government beyond voting. Whatever we have of the genius of regulating behavior, trying to think of possible plans (as opposed to the ideal plans priests and artists are always laying before us) and trying to sell workable ideas—the whole course of government—we aren't using it much. Carl Jung warned over and over against not using creative gifts if you have them. Dr. Marie-Louise von Franz warns over and over that these unused creative gifts turn to "pure poison." Dr. Franz is a careful as well as eloquent scientist; her use of the expression "pure poison" is advised. If we translate "creative gifts" to "gifts in human government," I think it is clear that unused political gifts, too, turn to poison. In the case of unused political gifts, the poison is called paranoia.

Literally dozens of times I have seen intense anxiety fill the faces of people when someone has said something like "I think that the FBI had something to do with the murder of Martin Luther King." Now this possibility of involvement by the FBI in that death was in the press many times, yet it causes sudden pain. Why?

I think the reason is that we feel secretly guilty about not taking part in our democracy. Our rural towns condition us to being cheerful publicly—to cooling it rather than pointing out harsh truths—but we still feel that participating in government is part of being a human being instead of being a lion or a cow. So we feel a terrible anxiety when evil is done in public life, and we defend against the discomfort of it by saying: "Oh, you can't believe everything you hear!" "Time was, people were willing to love their country without all this negative talk but, boy, I guess not any more!" (again the end of the Golden Era) or "You hardly know what to believe any more, do you?" Every single one of those remarks begs: Please do not lay it on me about King, or Vietnam, or Third World mothers and their baby formula, or Watergate, or Allende's murder, or Korea. I was not told I'd have to bear those griefs!

Another defense-mechanism remark interests me more than any of the above because it has a solution. It is: "Yeah, but if you once get started with all that protest business where's it all going to end?" The cheerful reply is: You can start or quit fighting evil at any time, and decide specifically which evils you will fight, on any timeline. Only fantasy work is without measure and forever—like fantasy enemies. Real work you can enter when you're ready, and you can plan exactly when you mean to leave it. The perfect practitioner of this was Jesus, who rebuked his mother at Cana for showing his hand beforehand (implying a timeline), who frequently "slipped through the crowd" instead of getting arrested because that wasn't in his plan for just then. Also, he instructed the disciples not to do anything until he sent the Holy Ghost to them. In other words, only fantasy enemies are on the field against you at all times.

Truth wins against political paranoia, I think, when we can split this plural, vague, inner-outer enemy *they* into its two parts: the real agent doing some real wrong to other people's lives for the sake of gain, and the huge, constantly flexing, shimmering body of our psychic fears. It means struggling for more consciousness in governmental things, the same struggle we need so badly in other aspects of rural life.

The irony of rural paranoia about what *they* are doing to us is that what real people are really doing to us is actually worse than the fantasies. Someone can sit on his front stoop and mutter about how *they*'re seeding Canadian thistle from airplanes so we have to buy 2-4D to kill it (that's one of the current ones) but what's Canadian thistle compared to the CIA's confessing (March 1977) that, well, yes they did do some germ warfare experiments in American cities.

When the fantasy-enemy action is chickenfeed compared to what real agencies are doing, it is time to become whole, politically, and identify an enemy head or two, and have at them. I think it would also bring a wide-awake feeling to our sleeping countryside.

# Ways Out: I.
# Non-Resource People

In the London Underground (subway) wherever you are, at no matter what oppressive lower level, you can see huge blue signs with the white letters that read WAY OUT. I mean to spend the next three essays thinking about the ways out of banal life in our countryside.

An early step taken by any new regional organization is finding out who the "resource persons" are in their area. These resource persons are identified by their wisdom, clout, or local community profile, and forever after are listed as "tools" available for furthering the "guidelines" and "goals."

Regarding people as instruments is not really disgusting; it is just unlikable. Any resource person can, if irritated, sabotage it neatly. T. S. Eliot is the definitive man on sabotaging one's image as a resource person. Years ago the Church of England fixed him in their mind as a religious poet, and some poor parish courteously asked him to speak. Eliot chose not to read poems or talk about poems; he gave them, apparently, a two-and-a-half-hour lecture on the characteristics, origins, and effects of either the death-watch beetle or dry rot (I'm sorry,

I've forgotten which) in the roofs of English churches. They never forgave him—but it served them right!

The fair or unfair treatment of resource people can be waived: the subject of this and my next two Letters from the Country is ways out for *non*-resource people.

What is a resource person? And consequently, a non-resource person? Simply, a resource person is someone with a *Weltanschauung*—a clumsy but accurate German word meaning a way of looking at life, a kind of philosophical vantage point. A non-resource person is someone who cannot get out far enough from the surface of daily life to get a perspective; he or she is unpracticed in philosophy, unpracticed in psychology, unpracticed in gathering any unity or theory about the endless data of life. All our lives are a marvelous, rich, incredible jumble of pure incident, with one mindless thing after another happening—mindless, that is, until we have a vantage point. If we fail, however, to connect all these incidents into some sort of comment on life, then we are non-resource people.

For example, one might ask: So what does that *mean* that La-Vonne keeps busting everything? Processing jars, the whole tray of communion glasses that time—and yeah, that one time she accidentally opened the present from her daughter's boyfriend to her daughter and it was some crystal thing for the Christmas tree and she busted that, even. What does it *mean?*

The non-resource person's reply might be "Goll, she's quite a LaVonne!" or "You just never know, do you?" or (worst of all) "What do you mean what's it mean? What's it supposed to mean?"

The responses above are all heart-breaking refusals to interpret life. The resource person, of course, would have been giving off interpretations like escaped steam. If a Freudian resource person: "Oh, I see it all! LaVonne envied her daughter's love affair and wished to destroy all the evidence of it! Opening that, and busting it, was hardly accidental!" Or a Jungian resource person: "Ah . . . ah . . . very, very m-m-m-m—incredibly interesting! How strangely these things always fall into place, don't they? Yes ... LaVonne wishes to *break* the religious or spiritual accouterments of our day—hence the communion glasses drop! Hence the Christmas tree decoration drops! Each event participates in this psychic drive ... !" And finally, if the resource person was a Naderesque reformer: "Typical! Typical! Typical planned obsolescence and deliberate manufacture and distribution of irresponsible products for the American people—the American people are helpless, damnit, helpless! in these manufacturers' hands. Canning jars you can't trust! Communion glasses—even communion glasses! out of the worst glass possible! Even things for Christmas trees, and everybody knows that kids do most Christmas tree decorations; those things bust in their hands."

(I have exaggerated the resource positions—but not a lot. These samples resemble much of what counts as analysis, counseling, or interpretation.)

What is sad is the difference in how much fun there is. It is much more fun to be an interpreter—to have a way of regarding LaVonne—than to have everything LaVonne does simply mean nothing. Wrong opinion is more fun than no opinion; it is more fun to feel that LaVonne needs help than to feel, "Well, you just never know, do you?" So the practical problem is how to stop letting the non-resource person get beaten out of having views on life.

What we need, I think, just to begin, is a mail-order service in every Minnesota town, or every second town at least. People simply don't know where to get ideas, or what there is to be got. They haven't access to serious theories; they have too much access, from drugstore bookstands and from TV, to junk-culture output—we all know that—but they have almost no access to what's good.

Some SMAHC (Southwestern Minnesota Arts and Humanities Council) resource person muscles the St. Paul Chamber Orchestra in for a residency—but the non-resource person, moved by the concerts, doesn't know that he can get a choice of recordings of serious Western music, with comments. A mail-order servant could put him onto Time/Life records subscriptions, or Spoken Arts, or Caedmon, or the Musical Heritage Society. No one in Minnesota towns knows about Publishers' Central Bureau, with its terrific offerings in now-unfashionable classics. Few know the *Minnesota Magazine.*

Let us suppose an energetic resource person gets in a speaker who says the children should read genuine, serious fairy tales, not jaded satires and wised-up takeoffs like those on TV or in Golden Press books at the supermarkets. But few rural Minnesotans know that the Dolch series of fairy tales from all lands—stories from Tibet, stories from India, France—can be ordered. They are not expensive, but someone—the mail-order servant—needs a membership in the Children's Book Council, or a copy of the Compton Encyclopedia suggestions for reading aloud to children, or something comparable, so people can do some follow-up when speakers come to town and tell us how to change our lives.

Norwegian-American parents who are endlessly reminding their children of their Norwegian background usually haven't any way of knowing that Pat Shaw Iversen did a marvelous translation of the Asbjörnsen and Moe fairy tales, the spine of Norwegian folk literature, and it can be acquired.

A few years ago the Madison Adult Education program sponsored a five-lecture series called "The Ideas of Freud and Jung and How They Apply to Life in Madison, Minnesota." It was a perfectly killing lecture series—funny, charming, friendly, and very succinct. All thirty-five to forty people who came took part—laughing, telling things from their own lives, without frigidity or fear, because they grasped that psychology is simply a body of truth which we all take part in. But, if a series like that were taken to every town in Minnesota, the problem would be follow-up. How would a non-resource person know that he could get *Modern Man in Search of a Soul* by Jung, or that much of his grudging, querulous dislike of this or that pressure has been described in *Civilization and Its Discontents,* or simply that we are not alone in our feelings?

A farmer I knew only well enough to join in complaining about drought once called me and asked if I could put him onto any naval history. We talked a long time, gradually pinpointing his interest. He had served on a destroyer in the battle of "The Slot" and wanted to read about it. I got a couple of books for him, missed getting him the best one because I didn't keep at it long enough—but the whole thing was a grateful moment for me. This man had the two requisites of culture: he wished to reflect on his experience by reading others' accounts of the same events, and second, he understood history when it happened to him. (He didn't mistake Guadalcanal for just another day's work.) All he needed was someone with access to a copy of *Books in Print.* Few rural Carnegie libraries keep Bowker publications such as *Books in Print.*

For less than $150 the mail-order servant in a town could have the equipment needed: first, a copy of *Literary Market Place;* second, *Books in Print;* one copy of just one issue of the *New York Times Book Review* (just to get the book-research classified ads), some *Whole Earth* catalogues, a Dover Publications Cash Order Plan. Then the servant would place a small ad in the local weekly paper:

> LET US ORDER BOOKS, RECORDS
> for you. No extra charge.
> By telephone or mail only.

When I was doing this, one year I ran an extra ad which asked if there wasn't some book your mother read you as a child that you wished you had for your children? The response was remarkable for a town of two thousand. It means people remember genuine art. TV ads moved *Jonathan Livingston Seagull* to the non-resource people of the world, while resource people were reading the paperback Narnia series. Grocery stores sell Golden Press books with their mostly mass-culture cute art, while resource people pick up Arthur Rackham's illustrated volumes of Grimm in Minneapolis. Nursing-home residents with eye problems get told by their pastors to listen to this or that devotional radio program; resource people know they can get the Library of Congress lists of cassette books or they can subscribe to *Choice,* a periodical recording service which takes things from serious magazines like *American Review.*

Most of us would enjoy belonging to a network of serious interest. We want genuine truth to share with one another. If we can't have genuine networks like theological or psychological associations, we are forced into phony ones. Why else, in our Midwestern loneliness, would we assume phony Southern accents, and cry, "Breaker one-nine? Breaker one-nine?" into our CBs? It isn't fair that non-resource people have such poor access to books, records, and conferences in which life is considered lovingly. I seriously commend to senior citizens or people with a half hour a day free at a desk the idea of being mail-order servants to their towns. I'd be glad to give the information I have to anyone interested in taking it on.

# Ways Out: II.
# We Are Sick of Bible Camp

We are not sick of Bible Camp because it is wrong, but simply because it is incomplete. Around the campfire people learn some of the joy of the unconscious. They discover, by the hundreds in Minnesota alone, and never forget it either, the life which evades reason, which carries morality in its saddlebag but gallops much farther; and when they sing

> The Lord of Love
> Has come to me—
> I want to pass it on!

they are not mistaken. The experience is simply not complete because *contentment*, as such, which American churches teach without teaching *discontent* with it, simply doesn't explain our crimes, our fears, our horrible inaccuracy in reading each other's feelings, the sheer hauntedness of our dreams—all the things of the unconscious, the thousand natural shocks to which Shakespeare knew we were "heir."

The churches teach contentment even though Jesus lectured against it. He said he would divide man from man, and that he came with a sword. That suggests that Christians are supposed to have some pain. We are starved for this pain. The fact that people are spending more and more weekends of their hard-working lives, and even precious whole weeks of too-precious holidays, going to conferences and retreats means that they wish to understand their discontent, social or internal. People in Duluth, St. Paul, and Minneapolis know about conferences to go to. They know the addresses of the retreats. They hear about who's running some kinky, perhaps, but helpful group somewhere. They know which writers' conference has the lecture on C. S. Lewis (Bemidji). Country people simply haven't this information.

Rural high school seniors will hear from Army and Navy recruiting teams, paid for by taxes, often permitted to promote during school hours; their high school counselors; Vo-Tech school representatives; and church representatives and service organizations. No one will give the high school senior any idea that thousands of Minnesotans alone are seeking "alternative" answers to our banal way of life by joining others in small, workable groups to discuss serious things over the weekend. No one suggests to these young people that weekends of serious thought and tolerance instead of competition are nearly always more fun than the "fun weekends" of ordinary American social life, that require so much Smirnoff and tonic to keep up the grins. No one tells young people that literally thousands of Americans are really trying to learn about human nature so that we ourselves, and, it follows, the nation, will be less brutal.

I'm afraid the 1930s principle of merchandise selling—that cheer, not sadness, sells—has been uniformly adopted by our churches. It makes discontent a secret from the people. It ends up that Madison, Minnesota, Methodists don't know about the Methodist Federation for Social Action's *Social Questions Bulletin*; Appleton, Minnesota, Episcopalians don't know about the Episcopal Diocese of Minnesota's Christian and Social Relations Department, or even about the Joint Religious Legislative Coalition in the Twin Cities, which presses hard on social issues in the legislature. Baptists in Montevideo and Appleton don't know about the tough organ of the American Baptist Church, called their "National Ministries," which delivers nononsense stockholder proposals at Union Carbide annual meetings, suggesting that Union Carbide cut out expanding activity in South Africa until that nation cuts out its insane cruelty to its black countrymen. Marketplace Christianity, or marketplace witness from any idealistic group, means recognizing *discontent.*

I think we need to have two pamphlets published: the first should be a listing of all the conferences and retreats in Minnesota and nearby states, for every given year, with addresses to write to, and a descriptive paragraph. Names of speakers should be given. The distribution must be such that *rural* people hear of it.

This past summer J. F. Powers, foremost writer of fiction about American Catholics, read a whole story aloud about a Minnesota woman who had a vision, and how embarrassing it was to whom, and how the Church handled it, and then he answered questions about his feelings toward the church. There should have been hundreds of Catholics there—yet rural Catholics, even the priests, tend not to know any of Jim Powers's stories. And they didn't know about the Bemidji Writers' Conference, so they couldn't tell their parishioners about that evening.

The pamphlets must describe the retreats and conferences honestly. If it's the kind of snob-ridden conference where the leaders are manipulative or all tangled in competition among themselves, outshining one another in their use of the subjunctive in dependent clauses, then the description should say so. If we are going to feel dumb all weekend, we need to know about that, too.

The second pamphlet we need should be a listing of alternative life ways and social activity for graduating high school seniors. Most of what young people hear now is what George Orwell bitterly called "Straight Scoutmaster," that is, "Stay clean-cut, get a job in Distant Early Warning systems or some similar democratic activity, and do not act suspicious of major corporation motives or you won't make any money"—all that sort of *realpolitik* dressed up as pro deo et patria.

The young people need the addresses of the *Whole Earth Catalogue* successors, the Jungian conferences at South Bend, yogi addresses in Minneapolis, the American Friends Service Committee's workcamp centers and how to apply, the address of that Lutheran camp way up in Alaska where you can live and contemplate if you will help with the building. They need the address of Nader's groups, they need the names of some of the futurists' book titles, the title of Michael Washburn's book that lists all the government and social organizations the author researched which try to change the world for the better. If we haven't the address of anything except the local Legion Post it is not our fault if we remain Girls' Staters all our lives. We need the address of Common Cause on M Street. Kids in Minneapolis know about BHA in food packaging; kids in Madison don't know, still, about refined flour and refined sugar, although by now I bet there are people in California nursing homes eating miso. We need addresses like that of the publishers of *Diet for a Small Planet*.

If we had two pamphlets, something along the lines suggested above, I think we would have much more of a WAY OUT in Minnesota—a way out of unconsciousness; a way out of being fools through ignorance.

# Ways Out: III.
# The Way Out of Small-Town Niceness and Loneliness

In this last of three essays on Ways Out of some of the griefs of rural life, I'd like to apply some ideas from chemical-dependency therapy. I'd like to apply them to rural loneliness.

We have Sherwood Anderson, Johan Bojer, Knut Hamsun, and Ole Rölvaag to tell us that we've never been alone in our loneliness, but misery loves a cure a lot better than company. We have Hamlin Garland to tell us rural loneliness is unnecessary if you've already developed a taste for truth, but scarcely anyone reads Garland any more, and you have to have had some success in dealing with loneliness just to arrive at Garland's starting place.

I am not an alcoholic, but one of the most engaging books I've ever seen is *I'll Quit Tomorrow*, by a Minneapolis priest of the Episcopal Church who is also the founder of the Johnson Institute for chemical-dependency treatment. I would like to quote one paragraph of Vernon Johnson's and then shamelessly apply its ideas to rural loneliness.

It is our experience that working with the good feelings during the early stages of therapy is next to impossible. They are simply overridden or overlaid by the bad, which always appear first in therapy and must be modified before the more constructive emotions can become available at a characteriological level. This fact speaks to the counselor's approach to the patient. If he is accurately empathetic with this condition he will know the futility of approaching the chemically dependent by cajoling or appealing to his positive side in any way. If early on, for example, he says to the patient: "You're really a good guy!" the patient, while he may smile and mutter his thanks, will be put off. He will be thinking, "Either this guy doesn't know me at all or he doesn't know this disease, or he is after something!"

Let's say a lonely small-town person is in the same spot, only nearer center on the continuum, within the normal zone, and without the physical dependency. If he complains of loneliness, however, to groups in town, he will very likely be told early in the first interview, "You're really a good guy!" It happens in Kiwanis; it happens in charismatic prayer groups; it happens in some church counseling sessions. So, like the alcoholic patient, he is put off, because he, at least partly, knows that this assuring someone they're good is the very stuff of the small-town insincerity that makes us all feel so isolated. We shall somehow have to start—if we really mean to cure the loneliness—by getting rid of any lying we come across and can recognize.

Very nice Midwestern women tell their children constantly to (1) be nice; (2) think nice things; (3) and if you can't say something nice don't say anything at all.

We have more socially mute people in the Midwest than other sections have. It is perfectly possible that everyone is checking, unconsciously: "Is that something nice I was about to say? If not I won't say it." Somehow, we're going to have to get mothers to teach their kids to try to say what they really feel, or not to say anything at all. It will be an uphill battle, because mothers are very keen, especially in the Midwest, on bringing up their children with minimal use of four-letter words. But anyone who has ever been to any therapy group knows that four-letter words are somehow part of the *modus vivendi* of dismantling repression.

The first of the mother's advice to her child is fine: be nice. Or better: be good. We really do need to be good—to stop knocking over small store owners' shops, to stop speaking rudely to people, etc.; but the second and third—*think nice things* and *say only nice things*—are appalling. They are a malignant mix of repression and hypocrisy.

It is a terrible pressure to put on children—that Minnesota mothers are so nice and want their children to be so nice. New York mothers really do not require niceness of their children. Minnesota mothers find a lot of niceness in the environment; they respond to the environment by insisting their children meet it with still more niceness. The New York mother finds a lot of real hostility and violence in the environment and she responds by showing her daughter sóme things you can do with your heels in an A train if someone gives you any grief at rush hour.

In the passage quoted from Dr. Johnson, the alcoholic has one of three responses to the counselor's positive remarks: (a) this guy doesn't know me; (b) or he doesn't know this disease; (c) or he is after something. I'd like to dismiss (c) first, as a necessity of the marketplace. In a town of 1,500 or 2,000 we are all necessarily selling one another our products. I can hardly expect a man who is trying to make me choose a Fiesta over a Chevette or vice versa to initiate an encounter session with me. And there are people in town I will never offend if I can help it because they are key people in the projects I care about. The marketplace is always with us. There's no good in shedding tears over it. But, if you read the word "disease" as "loneliness," then in (a) and (b) you have the recurring feelings of small-town people a dozen times a day. This guy doesn't really know me; this guy doesn't really know how I'm suffering.

We shall simply have to get over the constant lying about feelings. Lonely people go off to prayer groups and repeatedly get into the same lying about feelings. The classic recurring example is the person new to the prayer group who says something like, "Yes, but if God is so wonderfully omnipotent—and you all seem so wonderfully confident, as if he's taking care of you—" whereupon heads nod enthusiastically "—then why did He allow Buchenwald and Auschwitz to take place?" The answer always comes back something like "We can't understand His ways . . . but everything works to the good," or, in the orthodox Christian response: "There is evil in the world as well as good—a buildup of it." But both opinions, no matter how reassuring they appear, take no serious account of those millions of deaths by gassing, shooting, and torture, and both opinions ignore the *feelings* of the person who asked the question. The loneliness redoubles.

The current fashionable response to rural loneliness is to bring in good art. Thanks to the lively regions, the Minnesota State Arts Board, the foundations, and local cultural-affairs committees, the serious music has arrived; the tough, beautiful poetry is here to be heard; and exhibits from Minneapolis museums are occasionally trotted around to be seen. It is lovely for people in enough contact with their feelings to be nourished by them.

For the people brought up by a Midwestern nice mother, however, serious art is more problem than nourishment. I've watched serious art fail for years. I would like to see the local committees inquire in the Twin Cities about what's available in group leaders who could come out on a weekly basis, work in groups of ten, in three-hour sessions, for ten sessions—and then begin with another group of ten. Here is why: we are isolated by negative feelings, lack of self-esteem, conflicts between our ideals and what we really bring off. Only a good group can set up a society for us where we can learn to recognize these feelings and speak them. In our town of 2,242, forty-eight people go to AA and Alanon; behind each of them stand between two and three, AA members assure me, who should be there. If all these went, there would still be over 2,000 people who have literally no place to go where they don't have to think nice things and say nice things.

People think they haven't a right to join a group unless they have an "emotional" difficulty. I suggest that local cultural-affairs committees, unless they're just trying to make their town arty, should try to show everyone that our niceness-cum-avarice culture literally causes emotional problems and that it is so strong—we are so wedded to saying-nice-things-or-nothing-at all—that we need intervention from the outside. If we got groups going in rural Minnesota among "normal" people, I bet much of the loneliness supposedly endemic to country life would disappear in a fortnight.

# Back at the Ranch, Small Dragons, Small Princesses

---

*A Minnesota man had three sons who came to him and said, Father, we are grown now; give us your blessing, we're going to stay around here.*

---

How different it is to be the middle-aged parents of grown sons and daughters in the 1970s than it was in the 1950s and early '60s! Then, nearly all young people "of promise" left the farms and small towns. They left at eighteen or twenty-one, depending on how much training they chose after high school. The important point, from the parents' side of it, is that they left.

They brought back their unsettling new ideas on the weekends, such as: there may be a more civilized way to run a funeral than to expose a corpse in the narthex; or heavy lunchboxes of sugary foods at 9 A.M. and 3 P.M. in the fields may not be good nutrition for hard-working men; or covering the medical costs to a seventy-year-old in pain from a terminal disease will not destroy American initiative.

They brought these unwelcome ideas back on the weekends, but the parents knew that sooner or later late Sunday afternoon would come with the sky orange and cold behind the bare groves in the west, and Son or Daughter would drive back to the Twin Cities. When they left, the parents sighed and proudly returned to their own values, such as a hard day's work for the pay; singing without feeling dumb at Kiwanis Monday noon; no padding expense accounts; Mom doing the dishes (Dad never did them; he had his own work); not feeling guilty about not writing Congressmen.

Cultural backwash means cultural backwash, with the advantage of firm values to sustain and the disadvantage of firm values to smother you. Parents who dread vandalism, dope, and cheating are grateful to relax in the backwash. When Son and Daughter left for the city, they took their new, unnerving values with them, and if their parents missed them, at least the very fact they were gone meant they were doing the world's work on a high level: destroying such dragons as want destroying, seeking out some princesses worth saving.

The *landesflyktning* is over now, however, and we have a small new kind of population living in our countryside. We have single men and women living alone or together on run-down abandoned farmsteads, the acreage of which is being worked by the regulars. There is a small, foreseeable confrontation between these intellectual or artistic renters and their landlords. The landlord says, "Ja, I guess you can sure live there if you want, until spring anyhow, and then Cordell and Mervin are going to push that grove down and wreck the house and put the whole thing in straight crop." The two men regard each other in moral shock. The renter deliberately shows that he thinks it is appalling to push down a whole grove of trees as if their lives counted for nothing holy. The owner deliberately shows his shock that a healthy and apparently smart man in his twenties should be willing to live in a dump, eschewing carpeting and indoor plumbing in favor of wooden floors (which went out with Laura Ingalls Wilder) and an outhouse with a Virginia Woolf poster on its door.

In Lac Qui Parle County we have a sprinkling of now ten,

now fifteen, young people living in abandoned farmhouses making pottery, writing poetry, devising beautiful room dividers and Venetian blinds of cornstalks, barn joists, and much else their eyes see beauty in. They read Jung and Doris Lessing and *Alive and Aware*, and four of them belong to Amnesty International. A few of them patiently go to the churches in our area, but instead of subjecting themselves, mute and paralyzed, to liturgy and sermon, they tend to make weird "creative" offerings—they help the Sunday school kids make better-worked banners than they would bother with otherwise.

When the church feels confident enough, it can make surprising use of intellectual young people. An Episcopal church in Swift County had a talk one Sunday in 1977 in which the lay reader passed out handprinted copies of William Blake's poetry so the whole congregation could read and think along while he spoke. But even churches that would feel threatened by that kind of format usually welcome artistic efforts.

Still, these artistic or intellectual young people are a little embarrassing to their parents. They have, for one thing, very strange priorities in people. They are disrespectful of the post commanders and often of the pastors, yet they will spend hours taping both coherent and incoherent Lutheran Home residents old enough still to speak Norwegian. They prize the old way—whatever it was. There is a grateful relationship between these young people and the old people they listen to. Both sides are careful to call Trondheim by its old name, Trondhjem. Both recognize, and somehow still bow to, the heaviness that entered the heart of men and women who carried all their possessions into steerage a century ago. If the young people are making any mistake in this oral history recording, I suspect it is in putting too much value on stunning anecdotes like children's births and deaths in snowstorms, and not enough value on philosophical truths learned by the old. Thought is more serious than data—at least, sooner or later one wants to honor it.

This brings me to my next idea, which is that much of the alternate-life-style living going on in the Minnesota countryside right now does not mean engaging any very serious dragons. If we are throwing clay we are not lobbying for environmental hope. If we are living with little cash turnover by doing a lot of canning and dry preserving (which take time), we are not in Minneapolis organizing planning retreats on the cash economy. Generally, Minnesota farmers do little to influence the legislature for justice outside their own farm-marketing interests; the new artistic or intellectual element also do very little. The air full of cold and snow informs each day with beauty; if one is here enjoying it, one does not think very much about Steve Biko's comrades.

The presence of artists in the countryside adds a third stream to our culture. Now we have:

1. Our young people forming the cadre that will service the farms, the gas stations, the repairs shops, and the stores (as before);
2. The ambitious young who leave in order to bite off a greater chunk (as before); and
3. The new element: people returning after college to take up the simplest, usually part-time work, and to live private lives of some delicacy.

This last lot are causing their parents the first confrontation in thirty years between the old values and the new ones. In not leaving home after the weekend, but staying around all winter, they confront us with an idea category that is called "real negative stuff." Real negative stuff is any criticism of current attitudes. The young people keep making the following "real negative" remarks:

> Money is not an adequate goal for a life's work.
> Commercial food is now dangerous, and, Mom and Dad, you are asking for arthritis if you don't get off . . . (and then follows a list of center-aisle products).

> Dad and Mom, do you think you could restructure your
> evenings to be more creative than sitting in front of the
> tube, or at least watch the Appleton education channel
> instead of the Whatsit Show?
>
> Dad, try to imagine our soil as having a life of its own, full
> of microorganisms that need nourishment, instead of
> just a carrier between selected chemical fertilizers and
> your cash crop.

If this third element in rural Minnesota begins to approach
our community groups in any numbers, they will bring us discomfort, learning, and a welcome voice to confirm our suspicions on many subjects. If, however, they settle for merely private lives, they'll have no particular impact. Come spring,
Merv and Cordell will push over their grove without a qualm,
knowing they're just nuts. Their parents will half-consciously
perceive them as the Ivans of the fairy tales, who stay dusty
and warm at the back of the stove while other people's boys go
out to kill dragons. Now, all the world knows that killing dragons—more than getting a job in the cities—is a flashy form of
social climbing; one does it to make social contact with a prin-
cess—but still it is not slothful. It means a first, second, and
third son matching wit and wrist with a major evil.

My hope for the prairie is that artistic young men and wom-
en will join forces not so much with regional arts organizations
as with the status quo organizations. We could throw in our lot
together.

Turgenev understood the futile, hostile idealism of men in
their twenties in conversation with their parents. The classic
setting is the young man's visit home after years of sophisticated education. He insists on arguing his reforms with his father.
The old man listens, pretends to be concerned or dismayed—
whichever will please the angry youth—but the fact is he can
scarcely understand why the boy makes himself so unhappy.
Rural alternative-culture people waste such hours quarreling
over stone-ground whole grain with their dads! Is dad a big

enough dragon to conquer? I should like to see the young instead approach the existing bakery in town and work out together a plan for promoting and marketing organic bread. Losing one's temper with the old folks is small beer compared to figuring out a way for alternative culture and existing merchants to cooperate.

# Brethren Too Least for Country Life

*Inasmuch as ye have done it unto one of the least of these my brethren, ye have done it unto me.*
—St. Matthew 25:40

Every idealist or conscientious organization at some time invites unsuitable people, people they regard as the least of brethren, to their hearth to offer (as well as kindness and skill permit) some kit for a better life.

East Coast prep schools work hard to get kids of parents who despise liberal-arts ideas. Andover, for an example, has tried especially to make a place not only for inner-city kids who somehow have Andover ideals, but also for redneck kids who decidedly have *not* got Andover ideals. Schools make this effort not just for the federal funding but because they want to give a leg up to the children of coarse or feckless adults.

Trying to help sociologically less blest people is as old as its reverse—slumming. For every Prince Hal upending a few with soldiers incapable of staying sober even on patrol, there is another Hal inviting a scoundrel's son and ne'er-do-well's daughter to the family place at Battle Lake for the whole summer—and meaning it.

*95*

What makes someone underqualified for small-town life in Minnesota? The determinant factor for the woman of the household, anyway, is whether or not she can *serve*. (Serving doesn't mean the Navy or someone's kitchen in Edina or Rye, by the way: it means putting out the coffee and marshmallow bars for blood-donation days at the armory, flu-shot days at the Home, Legion auxiliary, etc.) It isn't easy to *serve* in a rural town. You have to be able to make lists, to show up on time where you said you'd be, to be trusted with the Sunshine Fund in cash without someone thinking you'll hie off with the odd quarter. You can't be so slovenly groomed that people won't work with you.

I don't think there is too much a town can do if both members of a household are content to sleep it off after the big quarrel or the big drunk Saturday night. But if one of them, and for convenience's sake, let us say the woman, very dearly wishes to be invited to zip on the Protestant robe or button up into the Episcopal cassock and puzzle out some Vulpius in choir—if she wants that, then we must figure out how to get her there and keep her there.

I am always cross at myself and other Minnesota writers for being so enamored of Scandinavian rustics. We repeat to one another, richly, their rough remarks at their deathbeds (not that I haven't the intention of getting off some memorable witticism at my own death, surmounting fear and pain in some gorgeous way); we write about their succinct philosophizing, which, we tell one another solemnly, a lot of these so-called pastors around here would do well to emulate—and so on. The gruff, stable Scandinavian we admire so much does not need us at all. There is a new rapidly multiplying element in our towns that does. Ten years ago no A.F.D.C. mother had a Madison address. Now several have. Ten years ago in Madison there were at any one time between four and seven people who wished to make the study-club-cum-church-circle scene but couldn't possibly because of being brethren or sisters too least. Now there are many more.

The one who needs help is that householder or adult member of a household who wishes to escape a shiftless, undignified, loud-shouting, unkindly life if only for a few hours a week. Her two objectives are: some humane exchange—no snarling, no beatings; and a chance the children might be accepted in town.

We have one unrecognized but marvelous rural institution that serves this person well. It is what's called out here "open houses." Open houses take place (in a good open-house winter) at intervals of two or three weeks at one merchant's store or another throughout January, February, March, mainly. The Peavey and the John Deere open houses are the best ones I've been to. What is good is that everybody fits. You wander into the store at any time of day and get some coffee and a cookie. People are standing around in ones and twos, so if you haven't a friend in town it does not show. You can come in bibs; you don't have to change into a sport shirt, which is important to farmers over forty. (The younger ones are used to wearing "matched work outfits.") Women don't have to change into their best double-knit pants suits. To save face, in case you are known to be lonely and taking whatever you can get for company, you lightly handle the cheap screwdrivers on sale in a bucket, but then you go briskly over to the displays of things *not* on sale to show you are a regular customer, not someone cluttering around all the open houses. The best thing is to come in fairly snappily, look round, and say, "That's right, I read in the *Guard* you had open house but I forgot all about it, chalk it up to age," and people laugh because we are good, in our town, at supporting any wit we can. Then, as briskly as you can, you go straight over to the expensive stuff—imitation colonial black-hammered hinges, say, for indoor cabinetry. When someone comes over to help you, you say, "I can't make up my mind which route to go—Early American or French Provincial," and then they say, although they know perfectly well you get all your furniture at farm auctions and then only if the bidding on the busted stuff stays under $10, "Take your time!

Have some more coffee! Think it over. Give a yell when you want help!" How nice that is to hear if you are sorely wounded from habitually rough domestic life; or from your complaining he doesn't make enough, his complaining the kids look dirty; or from some church-circle women, big shots, who snubbed you right from the next chair at Donna's Beauty Shop.

The John Deere Implement open houses are great because they clear out all but a couple of the huge tractors from their hangar-like shop, so tables can be set up and a movie shown after a noon lunch of franks and beans. It is very nice. We all sit down disorderly and talk to faces we have seen around. We tell each other, "I know I ought to know you but I just never was good at faces." The John Deere employees in their nifty green outer-space outfits serve us carefully. They don't slop the coffee and they don't skimp you. After a while they darken the shop and the son-in-law climbs up on the box of a Ford pickup, standing behind us like a green dragon robot, and projects a half-hour film of magical new 1970s equipment onto a screen. We watch, all of us, experts in the dark. All of us, even the very old women who know more about horse days than side-delivery snow-blow fronts, are experts; we know how to converse about the ghastly cash layout to buy this equipment versus using old stuff. And in the dark some of the heads are a little silhouetted in front of us.

We know these are all people who belong to us, and if some fool semi from up north comes down U.S. 75 and flattens us on the highway, these people will dig us down and sing "Fast falls the eventide" down-aisle from us. When the lights come back on, we, even those of us who haven't enough discipline to sew on a button instead of keeping a safety pin in our clothes, or a dime to buy a used zipper with, can carry on with dignity a conversation about diminishing returns in agricultural operational investment. The conversation is everything our home talk is not: it is relaxed, it isn't loaded, and it is mutually respectful. We remind ourselves that tomorrow Jackson's Super

Valu is serving baloney on toothpicks in one of the aisles and the woman who stands over the serving of it doesn't snub anyone.

This peripheral social life of open houses is a better aspect of small-town life than church-circle meetings. Men's church and organizational groups, too, don't work if you are a man perched between the layoffs at the foundry and the layoffs at the fertilizer plant. You can't expect to cast dice for the coffee and carry it off in that robust way the confident men do—the police, the businessmen. You're *out.*

I watched all one winter as a woman failed to make it in church circle and choir. She had had enough outpatient group therapy from a mental health center so she lived in an aura of friendly, open people. Then she came to our circle. One morning she came late and said in her always too-loud voice, "Yeah, I got here late because *he* said you ain't going nowhere until you scrub the whole floor end to end and I'm sitting here to see you do it too, so I did it, because he can get real ugly if he don't get his way, but then I got dressed and here I am." I would like to report that all the other women simply froze, and the Harvard Psychology Department, which is dead keen on behaviorism, could perfect hundreds of methods of negative reinforcement if they could see how we treat people desperately striving to become middle-class. It takes a careless social worker to send an outpatient to a women's circle meeting.

I've thought of only the feeblest ideas for improving the situation. First, we could change the ratio of therapeutic groups to *nice* groups in our towns. We could halve the auxiliaries and circles, and double the family-life seminars, adult-education courses out of the high school, AA-related activities, and the one-shot ad hoc groups that do parades. My second proposal is that rural writers, who are pouring into the countryside nearly as quickly as indigent families are, help the townspeople to open the respectable activities to unsuitable people. That is, instead of always relegating the tough lady to the church kitchen to pare carrots, let her be a waitress right out upfront at the fair stand. She won't wreck it completely. Let her mumble through choir; one monotone soprano will not ruin a choir more quickly than twenty slothful tenors and basses, and all rural choirs deal amiably with slothful tenors and basses.

Let's press the whole town to let anyone be respectable who aims at it, no matter how badly they do it.

# Turning Plowshares
# Back into Swords

I remember marching in St. Cloud one afternoon, protesting the Vietnam War. Behind me and ahead of me were St. John's prep students and some old regulars out of Minnesota's anti-establishment stable. How I hated that march at first! I didn't feel respectable any more and the pedestrians of St. Cloud gave us such looks. What got me over the hump was a big rich black car that got to cruising slowly past us; when ahead, it would gun up power, race around the block, and next thing we knew, there it was, slowly cruising along us from the back again, windows rolled up. Behind the windows a lot of big guys glared at us. Finally, about the fourth time around, one of them lowered the window and shouted an obscenity at me. The obscenity had to do with my grandmother.

For hours I could not imagine why I felt so stunned by that. Then I saw what it was. I was not just a nice woman you couldn't point at any more. I had become political, and the moment one becomes political one becomes visible, of course, to one's enemies. A queer little chill went up my back. It was like the chill growing children feel when they realize life is going to happen to them themselves, including that part of life called death, at the end.

It would have been nicer to have a more elegant enemy. We would all rather have a whack at a huge green dragon and then have the town crier run around later shouting, "Now you may all come out of hiding!" But any enemy will do for starters. Mine was a fifty-year-old who was even more chicken than I was. It took him four times past our group before he could even roll down the window and croak out some square-one obscenity.

The American Agriculture Movement farm strike brought back this memory because now thousands of farmers, not just leaders, but both leaders and followers, are having to stop being just nice people you don't point at. Despite our Minnesota liberal past, most farmers have escaped thus far the horrible discomfort of taking up for one's own interests against the powers that be. The regional leaders of the A.A.M. in my area have a no-nonsense and sensitive grasp on that pain. One of their speakers, Ann Kanten, said in Madison: "I am wearing a strike button. I have a problem with this word *strike*"—and she went on to describe how farmers have always been told to *bear* it, whatever was wrong, not to *right* it. Another strike leader, John Cairns, said: "We love to farm! We love it. People who think we want to go to the cities are wrong. We love doing it— preparing the fields, all of it. In April, when those fields look right to us, and we know they're right, it's the right time, we're going to want to go out and work up and plant." In other words, both speakers, while urging men and women to cut their crop by 40 or 50 percent, were also stating a sophisticated psychological fact: there will be agony in acting politically.

Man is *not* a political animal—not naturally. What he is naturally is the comfortable son of his parents. The easiest thing to do in life is to stay a son or daughter all your life—loyal, filial, trusting of authority. First, the parents to whom we are son or daughter are our real parents. Then we are son or daughter to

(1) our parents and (2) our teachers. Later we are child to our teachers and our government. If we are religious, we are child to our government and our god, even though Jesus was furious at people tied to the parent image. Naturally, painlessly, we are a son or a daughter of something parental all through life. How much more comforting to believe that God will help through prayer than to realize that Minnesota's Congressmen and others held off the Ag Land Fund (a brokers' plan for Midwest land acquisition and subsequent sales) for the moment, but there is a huge stockbroking establishment with its Congressmen that still and always wants to turn the Midwest into a realty-investment source. How much more comforting to think shopkeepers and middlemen "leach along the way" on prices than to face the brutal fact that men and women more than a thousand miles away are deliberately lobbying to get us and our kids off our family farm. Being political is an acquired quality, for better or worse. We don't ease into it.

There are two other reasons why political awareness is hard for Minnesota farmers. One is historical. In leaving Hardanger and all the Vestland of Norway, and all the provinces of Sweden and Finland, men improved their lot by flight from rigid, inimical governments and by hard physical labor. It worked, too. Obviously it was the right solution for nineteenth-century European agricultural griefs, but the psychic fact, I feel, is that it left imprinting in our group memory, so that when in stress one can turn one's back on any specific enemy and then make up one's manhood feelings by just terribly hard work plus a stoical attitude.

The second reason is one I discovered in breastfeeding my children. One of the greatest pleasures in life is to be doing some kind of work, like caring for a baby, and then to *keep on doing it without changing mood*. You nurse the baby, hold it awhile, lay it in its safe place to sleep, go out and get in wood for the fire for the living room its family sits in, cook meals for its father and brothers and sisters, then wonderfully, incredibly, heavily, as if the whole clock turned around it comes time to nurse the baby again. All day and half the night the heart and mind have moved together in one mood, mothering. How much easier to read aloud to the older children those evenings, stalling around for the ten-o'clock feeding of the baby, than to drive uptown to a meeting about strontium 90 or iodine 131 or some other damnable thing being perpetrated by some Americans on millions of other Americans. I am an expert at ducking out of political work.

A little field work showed me farming is much the same: you long to linger at whatever job you are doing. From the first swiping the dew off the tractor seat in the morning farming is absorbing, utterly interesting. Flopping down on the scratchy headlands at nine and three to satisfy the great Minnesota caffeine hunger is absorbing, utterly interesting. Then at night my half-numbed feet leap away from the familiar clutch and brake pedals to be shocked by the stubble and clods of the ground. (There is a tottering about after you have been plowing all day.) Even that is absorbing and utterly interesting. And if you are doing field work it is unpleasant to change to grove-and-farmyard work; and if you are doing farmyard repairs it is hard to change to the thicker air of the house. And, when you are doing canning, those big unscented fields out the window look so stupid and coolly masculine; it is these spices that are lovely!

All farm people have had the experience of repairing something at some far corner that one doesn't usually pass. It is especially pleasant to work in some unwonted place. I remember putting up steel fence for pasture. At the far southwest corner I came to a thirty-foot area where I couldn't auger holes for the fence posts: the ground was solid rock, beginning about a foot under the surface. I resigned myself to the extra work that meant. I bought cement, brought over the wheelbarrow and other tools, mixed concrete, and set the posts in it. After a while the grass was trampled around that place; my tools looked right, lying there; the wheelbarrow full of mortar mix looked like everything in Genesis before anything was anything—*it* looked right. A part of me wanted to linger in that corner of the farmyard where I had given some devotion. That part of me didn't want to go uptown and try to get people to cooperate with Southern farmers in cutting back 1978 crop production. We long to stay in the fabric of nature, in the fabric of privacy, even in the fabric of physical exhaustion. We long to rub off politics with "God'll fix it."

People are always praising farm families for *enduring*, because then those families are being trusting children of the system. How childlike it is to say, "Well, I guess He works out everything for the best in His will!" And how pleasing that is to nice ladies and nice men! And to not-so-nice people that cruise in big cars past every strike of any kind.

# The Last Person to
# Get a Grant

First, the grants for research went mainly to universities on the East and West coasts. Academic people got everything. Money even went to "institutes" for "humane research," at least one of which turned out to house a chemical warfare laboratory. Hundreds of professors and instructors got grants to finish private research projects. Grants also went to universities and private corporations jointly, whose effect was to subsidize the corporations' research. Grants went to businesses to develop products which later were contracted for by government agencies at top prices.

Grants eventually went to social science and humanities scholars all over the country, and, in the third stage, to individuals who had some paracultural project going in which the local community was to be involved on some level. Soon a generation of thirty-year-olds knew how to write grant applications and middle-aged men and women who had been associated with steady employment in management got used to picking up three- and ten-year positions as "project directors" for institutions receiving grants.

The last person to get a grant is going to be the Minnesota farmer, but it looks as if his time has come. It is one of the ironies that he is the last subject of consideration because he "fits all the guidelines for need" better than nearly everyone else:

1. He is in despair because economically and psychologically his way of life is not working.
2. He has no political friends in his campaign, unlike the women, who had allies in the anti-Vietnam War movement because they had worked together; the blacks, who had allies among the white liberals because they had worked together; and the environmentalists, who had immediate support from idealists and, oddly enough, well-heeled upper-class Eastern middle-aged and retired people who were used to owning beautiful land and wanted it kept that way. With few exceptions the farmer has been unpolitical for a crucial forty years. Keeping to himself on his quarter section in 1940 (which by 1950 had to be at least a half section if you were to "make it," and by 1960 often a thousand acres or better of corn, soybeans, flax, and wheat), the farmer did not really pay any attention to movements of any kind other than those of the Secretary of Agriculture. His idea of political commitment was carrying a bumpersticker with a pun on Earl Butz's name.
3. He is not used to explaining his position or trying to see anyone else's. He has a full repertoire of phrases like "don't stick my neck out," "mind my own business," "big shots in The Cities," "can't tell how that'll turn out," and "there's nothing you can do about it anyway." Those are all remarks of unpolitical people who don't even think being political or social is particularly desirable. No wonder the humanities and arts grants go to tender-eyed young men and women who say they wish to fulfill themselves, express themselves, share their pottery, take their art to this group or that group, and whose "impact statements" begin cheerfully with conjectures like "actu-

ally one of the places this could go—if it really started rolling—is etc." They are more fun to talk to; they don't reply, "Hard to tell" to every question asked; and, most important, they knew the address of the grant donor and wrote for the application blanks.

I can't think of any more useful people to receive funds for discussions on ways of life than farmers. They have scarcely heard the issues nearest them addressed. They never get to hear really tough debate, with good thinkers fighting it out and caring on both sides, on any of the following:

> Paying farmers for crops by protein instead of by weight or volume.
> Chemical fertilizers vs. microorganism life in the soil.
> Dangers and advantages of cloud seeding.
> Opposing the technological bent of our high schools.
> Towns organizing into small cells of wind-power and solar-energy users.
> Joining one-shot social projects as a way of community service instead of belonging to service organizations and other established groups.
> Using or not using Minnesota water tables for irrigation.

All project proposals begin with the assumption that we haven't been doing something right. As groups like Southwest Minnesota Arts and Humanities Council are starting up discussion evenings in rural areas, the unspoken assumption is that something has been either missing or wrong. What, exactly? I think it is this: Much that makes life satisfying has been simply shrugged off by the Minnesota farmer now in his fifties.

He abdicated political involvement on a really fighting level almost before he started. Membership in the Land Bank and indolent attendance at Farmers Union meetings don't really constitute the American's right to fight through channels for his right to happiness. I don't think Jefferson and Wythe could have guessed at the apathy with which this group of Minnesota (and other) middle-aged farmers regard their chances as lobbyists, referendum starters, and protestors.

The farmer abdicated from a philosophical, informed view of life in general, partly because English—which is for high-school-educated people the main source of philosophical thought (the only introduction to it, often)—is taught so appallingly *technically* that the reading of great stories to see what life is—what love is like! what travel is like! what the mad passions of life are! what the enduring traits of character are!—all those for some reason slithered like oil between the cogs of getting people to stop saying "ain't" and "uh" between sentences when they were standing up in front of the class.

Also the Protestant churches aren't generally much good in rural areas for showing people a generative, respectful way to look at life because they are shrill and nervous about sin. Anyway, they are boring, too, like the English courses in high school. The farmer has, finally, given up having a really good feeling about himself because the way he made a lot of money in 1945–1956 doesn't work now, and it feels—in his lack of acquaintance with the workings of the American economy—like a personal failure of his own.

If paranoia is indeed the cutting edge of social justice, as George E. Vaillant writes in *Adaptation to Life,* the farmer would have to be a raving paranoid to get to work by himself on his three losses listed above—governmental instinct, philosophical ease and joy, and feelings of self-worth.

The bright side of this is the amount of attention rural America is now receiving from humanities organizations. It couldn't come at a better time. We will consider nearly anything. Ten years ago we would have called these soft-eyed and well-spoken grants people from the outside "some city people from somewhere," if we were not offended, and "some kind of Communist, probably" if we were. That is all changed now. Every direction really is up—a little steeply at first.

# A Malaise for Followers

*At the end of the seven years, Hans went to the silver-smith and said: "Master, I would like to go now and see my aged parents." The silversmith said: "You have worked faithfully and you are going to be a great worker in silver." The old man kissed the boy on both cheeks and for his pay put such a lump of pure silver into his sack that Hans could scarcely carry it.*

—A. Reynolds, *Märchen*

Tradition and fairy tale warn us, however, that Hans was near-ly a slave; all the seven years he was bound he did menial work about the smithy, and likely scrubbed up for the mistress as well. Nor were masters always this kind—some failed to teach their craft; some beat the apprentices. But, even so, Hans would have known that the seven years were all he owed and that in the end he would go off free, a better man than when he came because now he was skilled. And a better man in his own psy-che as well: he had been taught by a man of his own class, and was therefore not looked down on, the master's expectations for Hans being at least as high as his own. Hans learned the luckiest lesson in the world: when you take up a chalice to en-grave, you are a colleague of great smiths; just as when you pick up a watercolor brush you are a colleague of Constable; and when you rub resin on your bow—even if an instant later every family pet chooses to leave the room—you are a colleague of Mozart. You have left forever the *petit monde* with its mindless envy.

In our countryside Merv and LaVonne generally have a very different experience: they are not apprentices—they are followers.

I am furious at myself for all of my adult years when I believed some people are naturally just followers. "Society needs someone," we are taught, "to run the assembly belts of Rochester and Detroit, and fortunately that repetitive and uncreative work is right for some people. They would be very threatened by anything else. They don't want responsibility."

In the assumption that some people are suited for passive lives we ignore a salient psychological fact: unlike Hans in the fairy tale, who feels himself a colleague of serious artisans, Merv and LaVonne are resentful. In fact, they generally (in Minnesota, at any rate) refer to leaders in virtually any field as *big shots*. They even resent anyone who writes letters to Congressmen; it seems presumptuous to them, because they understand that life is made up of *us*, who are followers, and *they*, who are leaders.

I don't want to go into leader-follower ideas in the usual sociological context: we know that all societies throughout all time have trained drones to man their assembly lines, to shoot whom they're ordered to shoot on Indian reservations or university campuses, to type the letters from the income-tax service in Pennsylvania congratulating Mr. Nixon on the skills with which his income tax was prepared. What I am interested in is the *inner* experience of the follower, which parallels the outer, cultural conditioning. Its symptoms are (1) passivity; (2) the recurrent belief that all things are easier and more delightful in the beginning (including life itself) and then subject to deterioration and eventual dismay, and (3) the inability to take joy in the accomplishments of those who are more successful.

I would like to take up the second of these symptoms because it is the only one that may seem surprising. People with high expectations are inclined to discipline themselves first and then enjoy later; people bent out of shape to be followers tend to take it easy at first, and only when the results reach small crisis proportions do they suddenly practice discipline. For example, the small children of followers are not bothered with being taught manners; they may do whatever they like at the table—until suddenly they are fairly revolting teenagers: then the parents jump on them with rage. The child's early pleasure at the table and later anxiety support the feeling of having lost a Golden Age.

Behavior modification methods used with certain rural first-graders exemplify Golden Age thinking, where all possible good is at the present or the present plus the past: the future can provide only threat of loss or loss. Every Monday each child gets ten tickets. There is no chance to earn more, even should you go to the teacher on Wednesday and explain that you have thought up something you call a "field theory" and might you share it with her? So you start as high as there is—and all you can do is hang on or lose. It is nearly symbolic of the passive view of life; you can only lose. Ironically, too, you lose tickets by failing to obey and failing to be quiet, both virtues being follower-virtues—that is, they support the authorities' needs for order at the expense of the individual's expressing himself.

Follower-thinking tells the soul that the future holds much to fear indeed. Dozens of intelligent essays have been written relating the puritan love of money, and belief in money, with an immeasurable fear of death and, often, of merely being around anybody who is dying. If America needs to produce sociological followers to run its assembly lines, it must also be true—on a horrible and different level—that it needs to keep intact its fear of death, and that to do this it goes on bending normal people into people afraid of life's eventual end. Intelligent and innovative people say frankly that they think the reason it is hard to get open discussions going in the countryside is that *we are afraid.* The death fear operates to suppress discussion of any serious uncertainties.

It is evil to say such fear suits large batches of people. It is evil, too, to deceive people with remarks such as "God wants us to be followers just as he wants some to be leaders." I remember one incident so appalling even a Lutheran congregation laughed. The pastor said it would be nice if we helped the custodians get the church cleaned up by Pentecost, and if any ladies felt that they would like to "serve the Lord in this very special way" would they sign in the narthex? He went on to explain that the very special way was to scrape the gum off from between the radiator interstices in the Fellowship Hall and from underneath the folding chairs. If we had been regarded as *apprentices,* like Hans in the fairy tale, the pastor would have said: "Let's clean up the church before Pentecost—particularly let us have volunteers for a three hundred percent disgustingly revolting job of scraping the bloody gum off the radiators—and then we will be free to make better use of the Fellowship Hall afterward." Then we would have been colleagues in life together.

Never before have so many different kinds of people and groups been saying: the self-image in rural Minnesota is poor and ought to be good. I don't believe any more that it is natural for some people to lack confidence in themselves. A bad self-image, if that is what we have, is to the soul what bound toes were to Oriental feet. There must be dozens of ways to stop any process so heartless. I will try to describe a few of them in the following Letter.

# A Gentle Education
# for Us All

Whenever someone says, with that marvelous air of casual expertise that we all assume so well, "Sooner or later, of course, we shall have to go on the four- or three-day work week," someone else instantly cries, "Oh, but *they* don't know how to use their leisure time! The crime rate will simply skyrocket in the cities, and out here [in the Minnesota countryside] they'll just be out racketing around on snowmobiles and speedboats, cruising the towns and polluting the canoe country and littering up the countryside!"

*They* will exercise, no doubt, all the feckless qualities of people with low self-image and low expectations. The *we* who feel so apprehensive are apparently the charter members of a Human Species Society whose membership committee has lately made the most extraordinary mistakes: we charter members tremble at the club's leaded windows, with our quiet, decent Scotches in hand, unable to block out the sound of the new members—the crash and guffaw of their inane chaff ("Hey, Louise, have a good time but don't do anything I wouldn't do!" "Watch it, Merv—you know women!" and all the rest of the

Protestant good cheer), the pathetic boasting ("What're you driving, DeWayne?"), and saddest, the sexual jokes that smoke and smoke, not from bawdry, but from unease.

So much for the conversations from *them*. What about *their* lifestyles? The granddaughters of the women who piled turkey and dressing and four pies and jars of homemade gooseberry preserves onto the church sawhorse tables now come to the county fair with pie-mix pies and to church suppers with very third-rate hot dishes based on fake Chinese noodles and artificially-flavored gelatin salads. The great-grandchildren of the fiddlers who brought violins into the sod houses of the pioneers and played on winter nights (Mari Sandoz and Hamlin Garland and Laura Wilder tell us) will not practice their piano lessons, and when the rural music teachers complain to parents, the parents reply—surrealistically, "Well, I hate to get after him about it because it might put him off music." Once, at a recital at which four pupils simply didn't know their pieces by heart, the music teacher explained that "music ought to be fun for them, so I don't get on their backs about practicing too much."

The *they*, whose jokes are empty, apparently do not work with a will at either community events or the arts. We know more about them. They do not answer their mail; they accept chairmanships of Chamber and church and citizens' organizations and convene the group only when nagged and cannot remember the agenda. When they are secretaries they forget the minutes. At the meeting at which someone named Einstein came as guest and asked for two minutes on the agenda in which he expounded about $E$ or $mc$, I forget which it was, the minutes reported this as: "The guest speaker was real interesting and there being no other business we stood for the final blessing."

All this second-rate behavior is no elegant moral breakdown in my opinion, but rather a result of everyone being told ever since the end of World War II that your image in others' eyes, as well as your own, had to do mainly with your vocation and your acquired property. Good schools bent to the task of making everyone a gray flannel suit to wear. The rural high schools bent to the task of equipping people with all the technical training they could. The other courses like English and languages became rather shadowy—something you studied if you meant to be a teacher. Everything was thought of in terms of *job*. All the time this phenomenon took place—say from 1945 to 1978—the old classic secret vein of a quite different education theory went on being mined in the old classic secret way: the lucky few were educated to be "all around" people. They read literature not to teach English but because Chekhov's enthusiasm is catching. They were educated for happiness. If you ask someone who has had a background in literature and the other arts and the sciences if he was educated for happiness he will laugh, of course, and pass off some remark about *universality* in literature—and how it is interesting to see the unity between physics and chemistry. Still, he is not telling the truth about his education partly because it sounds silly to say yes, I studied liberal arts at Hamline in order to be happy. The other reason for his not saying so, in my opinion, is that this kind of education is unconscious.

The principle of literature is devotion to the particulars of life. Chekhov, for example, is not particularly universal; he is particularly particular. Those dreadful soirées he describes, with the eighth-rate singer and the maundering violinist doing a Russian equivalent to "O sweet amaryllis" badly in one corner while people hunch over the samovar, counting on tea as a mood-changing drug to carry them until the piggery of a midnight supper later—this is *particular* information.

For some mysterious reason, being informed of how the others do things, how quietly other kinds of life are lived, how other molecules behave in quite other circumstances from the ordinary, raises the ego's joy! It is the secret agenda of the liberal arts conversation: that studying whatever is *other*, in a non-judgmental but simply curious, ready-to-be-amused sort of way, makes people happy. We should have guessed: there are thousands of little boys and girls who mysteriously fall in love with dinosaur books. They bring these awful Golden Book dinosaur books home and simply pore over the pictures. They bore us with distinctions between the thissaurus and the thatsaurus until our eyes smart. It isn't that they are going to be paleontologists: it is that they have learned, on their own, the ebullient feeling of having a look at something *other* than themselves—and in the process the self laughs. The laugh is a very different sound from the sharp snort of idle chaff. (Hey, Louise, don't do anything I wouldn't do!)

It isn't fair that a deliberately impractical education which examines the verities of human life should be such a marvelous help to the self-image or the general ego strength and yet be limited to the gentleman. For years and years liberal arts graduates have taken up the best jobs in America, while others, whose coursework promised upward mobility, have desperately taken "business" courses without any suspicion that they were running their race on the layby track. Now that jobs are less and less rewarding, and for the most part people in rural areas cannot get the jobs they want, it is doubly unfair to keep the schools headed toward job preparation. They could much better be teaching preparation for the other two-thirds of our lives.

This brings us back to the snowmobiler and the languid family dazed before the set, or the aging boys and girls affixed to the Honda saddle. Of course the self-image must be low because they have not been shown that the *whole* human personality is worthwhile. They recognize only their own technical competence as a value: they know they can sew a flap onto a Stearns quilted jacket pocket in 1.58 seconds and the pocket itself on in 2.3 minutes. But that is not enough value. The person I am all the other sixteen hours of the day—what value can I feel in that person if I have never studied liberal arts? I record those sixteen hours as throwaway hours, and from the age of eighteen, if not before, I proceed to throw them away.

If schools are to educate for sixteen hours per day of leisure time, what does that mean? I think it could begin with courses, given by local organizations and by adult education departments of high schools, on community dynamics. It will help to have the *topics* for inquiry local, but the literature read to illuminate them, classics.

This is the opposite of what is practiced generally now in rural Minnesota: most community education considers universal or classical topics and then brings to bear on them the works of local second-rate poets and essayists. Here is an example, for contrast, of a local topic, and of first-rate nonlocal writers whose work offers comment on it:

> Topic: The granddaughters of the women who piled turkey and dressing and four pies and jars of homemade gooseberry preserves onto the sawhorse tables now come to the county fair with pie-mix pies and to church suppers with third-rate hot dishes and artificially flavored gelatin salads.

Among the works that illuminate this matter are Leo Tolstoy's "The Death of Ivan Ilyich"; Fred Manfred's "The Chokecherry Tree"; Carson McCullers's "The Heart is a Lonely Hunter"; and James Joyce's "Counterparts."

Our own life is worthy of the best thought so we should go to the best writers on the subject. This idea alone, which is not generally practiced in our private lives or in our schools, would cheer the ego. The crux of it is not only the implication that we have a right to the great truths, but that somehow the *other* must enter our lives or we will always feel second rate. Present cultural habits in rural Minnesota, as elsewhere, revolve around and around the self:

Will I get a decent job?
Do people think I'm O.K.?

Gee, aren't they ever going to bring up something in this meeting that relates to my town?

Bronowski, whom we love for *The Ascent of Man*, says quite flatly in *A Sense of the Future* that we are *all* meant to be creative people: "to my mind, it is a mistake to think of creative activity as something unusual. I hold that the creative activity is normal to all living things. Creation is the finding of order in what was disorderly, and this is a characteristically human activity."

It means for us, I think, that *they* on the snowmobiles should be let in on the secret education kit which the gentleman has always had. *Their* kids have a right to schools that take the music and art programs seriously. Working with egg cartons and used 7-Up bottle caps to make collages of junk will not do; they have a right to watercolor paint and they have a right to be scolded for not practicing. The school system, which uses so many hours a day, has failed somehow to force a pass through provincial self-centeredness. We unconsciously feel we are being sadly equipped.

It is as if we asked for a horse to go on a great pilgrimage and somebody constantly brought up foundered mules with the explanation: "Well, this'll get you to Dawson, which is probably about as far as yer going anyway." Infuriating.

# Where Have All the Fifty-Five-Year-Olds Gone?

We are wiser about the departure of the young people than about the departure of the fifty-five-year-olds. It isn't hard to know the precise Sunday when the sixteen-year-old server, up to now so kindly lighting up, bowing, handing, censing, and snuffing, is about to quit. The censer is slapped down in the corner of the choir room, still sending up its rank curl; the server doesn't just step out of the cassock, he thrashes his way out of it, treading on the beautiful twenty-three buttons. When we look on inquiringly, he offers this brief theology: "That's it, boy! That—is—it!" We aren't stupid: we know he is off to fail or succeed at secular life. In another two years his face, familiar as an 880 runner or a forward, will disappear from the weekly papers, too. He likely won't reappear in rural Minnesota public life for another fifteen years, if ever, because he will have rightly gone off to succeed or fail at love and work.

We aren't nearly so understanding of our fifty-five-year-old town leaders when they fail us. I used to dismiss their gradual defection from all the old causes like Chamber and Norwegian national celebrations and Christmas julebokking and Arts Center melodramas with either of the two general explanations small towns offer: "Oh—them! You can't count on them for anything any more" or "I suppose they figure enough is enough."

It seems logical that younger people should take over chairmanships, etc., but there is one fact that has made me spend some time thinking about fifty-five-year-old leaders in volunteer organizations. That fact is that they typically do not bow out of community life graciously: they do it badly. They are angry. Instead of working well to the end, they spend two or three years dropping poison—derision, outspoken pessimism, and paralyzing incompetence—into the very organizations which once seemed to mean so much to them. Over and over we see the once-encouraging play director now saying, "Well, I don't think the town is up to doing anything this year," and the once-efficient committee clerk saying, "No way will I go to the trouble of Xeroxing minutes when no one reads them anyway!" And the once lively member of the retail committee saying, "Oh, I don't know, I think people are sick of shopping in small towns—we all drive to The Cities anyway—what's the use of a promotion?" A measure of this advent of sourness is the cards which the circle chairmen keep for each of the members of the American Lutherans Church Women. Here is a typical one:

1967–68  Real active
1968–69  Real active, gave Bible study once but said she'd rather not
1969–70  Real active, real willing to serve, like at funerals
1970–71  Chairman of the circle
1971–72  Not too active
1972–73  Not so active
1973–74  Real inactive. No Bible studies
1974–75  Real inactive and said would we not call any more, because she and Mervin just didn't have the time any more

1975–76  Real inactive, and when we called because there was
         a funeral that came up fast she was almost angry
1976–77  Didn't call her. Pastor did go see her though.

In that bare-bones record of loss is probably hidden a story
of personal disappointment. If there were no disappointment—if she had thought, at fifty-five or sixty, that her work
for the community had been as well received and fulfilling as
she had been led to expect—there would not be the spite and
sabotage suggested here.

I think it is a psychological form of *occult restitution.* St.
Thomas Aquinas noted that peasants who felt they were forced
to work too many hours on the lord's estate for what he paid
them tended to pinch the odd goose from the lord's flock and
snare the odd deer in the lord's park—but they stole, Thomas
realized with sudden interest, only up to the approximate level
of what they thought they had been done out of. He called it
an instinctive "occult restitution." We know the twentieth-century economic form of occult restitution—the padded expense
account, the shaved deposit slip: But what if the psyche itself
feels cheated?

In the early autumn mornings when we race into town,
there is hoarfrost on our earnest buildings with their fake man-
sard roof fronts and on the railings of the Royal Café where the
Cultural Affairs Committee is going to meet for breakfast in
two minutes. For just this moment the frost looks like the *om-
nium invisibilium*—the invisible realm that we yearn for—made
visible. It looks the more like that for its being transparent; it is
more delicate than snow. It sifts out to us—for just a second—
all the great yearnings.

I remember standing on the steps of the café thinking, I
won't always be taking minutes for this committee or any committee! *Some*time I am going to think about life and death and
I'm going to get to someplace where people will want to talk
about it! And then I grabbed the plastic-covered screen door of

the Royal and went in to the committee. We were practical and cheerful and safe in our community good will. The waitress said she hoped we didn't mind if she gave us a hard time, and when someone everyone knows in town walked in we all looked up and someone else said very loudly: "They'll let anybody in this place, looks like." The man who had entered looked pleased and said, "Shut up." It was very nice. It is nice to live in a Minnesota town of two thousand people and have some things to do together. But one reason it is no more than nice is that we can overlook, but we can't forget, what the frost reminds us of: things invisible which have nothing to do with getting the St. Paul Chamber Orchestra to do us some services out here. Sooner or later we will crave time to deal with those greater things.

So anyone who hopes to express the soul's interests through local community service is eventually disappointed. Two things become clear: first, the community cannot help us with our own feelings about getting older and eventually dying. And second, our work has been largely ineffective. Ernest Becker, in *The Denial of Death*, makes a marvelous point of Freud's discovery that people have a big part of themselves that wants to be led around by others. We *like* to follow a charismatic leader—it is an actual, nearly visceral pleasure. Now we will invade Poland, he tells us; or now we will bring culture to this town; or now we will go into a five-year solid-waste-disposal project with three adjoining towns. But Becker points out that being a follower isn't good for people and that sooner or later they will betray the leader. If the slightest thing goes wrong with his project they will snap turn about and cry: "Yeah, I never really did think that was much of an idea anyway!" And "I went along with it all right, but I won't say I ever really liked the idea!" Or—the classic *cri de merde* of the twentieth century—"I was just following orders."

The fifty-five-year-olds resent—however unconsciously—having been led away from the self. Their greatest difficulty, however, is the loss of selfhood which has taken place over all the years of community activity. Alas, it isn't true that when one is devoted to public service the personality is thereby nourished.

I think this is the explanation for the dropping of poison, which older middle-aged people so often do, into the very causes they once graciously forwarded. Such behavior seems more common among the mainstreamers than the loners. The eccentrics who replant wildflowers all over the county or show generations of children how to trim a tiny boat so it will cross the Lac Qui Parle by itself, or write books about how the North Pole is really a fifteen-hundred-mile-diameter hole filled with jungle animals and plants (one such book is being written in my county right now)—these mavericks and dreamers are immune to the infuriating disappointments of the extroverted Chamber of Commerce member.

Let's return to the sixteen-year-old. He has just done two life-saving things: he has briskly shed his cassock and cried, "That's the end of *that!*" and he has read a marvelous story, Daniel Keyes' *Flowers for Algernon*. Both actions are terrific for the spirit! There is nothing like rebelling against a religion which you have decided is ridiculous—especially against a religion so established that it has some accouterments' you can stomp, such as cassocks for the servers. And there is nothing like reading a story that supports your worst suspicions about how technologists treat the heart of man or mouse (Charlie Gordon or Algernon, in *Flowers*).

Shrewd churchmen long ago observed, however, that no sooner does a person's spirit make a break for it, so to speak, than the very next day the Devil comes knocking, and you have to fight for your new-won ground. In the case of the small-town sixteen-year-old: he won't actually hear from the Episcopal priest the very next day because Episcopal priests try to preserve Mondays as days off, but Tuesday Father Whatsit is likely to drop round and have a word with our escaper. He will point out that there is a lot of fellowship and community and honor in the church and once out of the mainstream of it, a person ... might become very lonely.... In other words, he will use social anxiety to sandbag the soul's new truth.

The pressure to conform and serve is enormous. Most small-town people give way to it, since there is almost never any pressure coming from the other direction. The boy or girl is sixteen, and chances are he or she will silence all inner voice, and obey all community calls to duty for thirty-five years. Fifty-five appears to be the cut-off age for community life. We can translate the saw "You can't fool all the people all the time" to "You can deaden people's inner life for just about thirty-five years, not forever." Then the resentment emerges, and with it, the occult restitution.

# In the Same Bottle, a Different Genie

A natural problem of living in the country is that one is always behind the times. I have just become fascinated with *passivity*, now that that subject is so stale that all the conferences on it, all the workshops and seminars, have moved on into the Dakotas. I knew that would happen. It was the same with death-and-dying. I got interested in Sandol Stoddard's *The Hospice Movement* and Ernest Becker's *Denial of Death* at the point when Twin Cities friends assured me they were passé. Presumably we will soon be told that sexuality is out, absolutely out, and we mustn't give it another glance.

I want to think my thought about passivity, late days or not. To begin with—simply making observations—it seems to me that passivity occurs when there are no boundaries of time or place. Morally speaking, passivity is a kind of parallel to the dispersal of energy in chemistry. It is a moral equivalent to the old artistic idea that talent grows by its very confinement in some respect—that the genie's strength comes of his confinement in the bottle. What if the genie-and-bottle image can help us in moral things? If we simply make the assumption that passivity (which is a form of moral sloth) occurs when there are no confining boundaries (of either space or time), it would be helpful to think of other things which depend upon boundaries. The two that come to mind immediately are playfulness and integrity. If there is a relationship between these three things of life—passivity, play, and integrity—we ought to be looking at it. Ours is an era of high passivity, marked by less play (our children are statistically less imaginative than previous generations of children, our adults more willing to watch performance of others than to participate in games themselves), and the lowest general level of integrity in most people's memory. Be that as it may, I would like to provide an example of how *confinement in the bottle* is integral to play and integrity, and the lack of such confinement integral to passivity.

A child's boundaries necessary to play are, in space, the doll-house walls and, in time, the pretense that there is no future time. In order to play at anything, children do this cunning process: they lock off the future. Say that Rick says, Let's play dollhouse. O.K., Amy replies, I'll be the mother and the police and the ambulance, and you can be the father, the street cleaner, and the welcome lady. O.K., Rick says, but that is only for ten minutes, then I get to be the police and the ambulance. Right away, because future time is considered, the play is killed. It is no good being the ambulance and the police unless you are the ambulance and police with no end.

This walling off future time is so essential to playfulness that it extends to cutting off *present* time as well. The great good of *Once upon a time* is its pastness: whatever follows is not still happening: it happened only once. That limitation is the bottle. On a single occasion, way back goodness knows when, a king agreed to sell out his faithful steward to the dragon in lieu of etc. etc. If you add, as those idiotic "relevant" children's TV programs so often do, "I bet you children know of similar things in your town, too, don't you? I bet you kids can name

*In the Same Bottle, a Different Genie*    **127**

some things that kings have—like, what does a king wear on his head? Can you name a country that has a king?" What such programs do is remove the boundaries of space and time in one blow. The genie's power is as dispersed as gas under pressure when the lid goes off. An unrecognized value of fairy tales is their containment.

Those are two of the boundaries of play. The boundaries of integrity are much the same, but more inner, more sophisticated. Here is an example from the life of Dr. Carl G. Jung.

At an early point in Jung's career he found that if in a certain research paper he did not give credit and credence to Freud for certain concepts his own career would be spared a shaking.

> "Important people" at most mentioned [Freud] surreptitiously, and at Congresses he was discussed only in the corridors, never on the floor. Therefore the discovery that my association experiments were in agreement with Freud's theories was far from pleasant for me.
>
> Once while I was in my laboratory and reflecting again upon these questions, the devil whispered to me that I would be justified in publishing the results of my experiments and my conclusions without mentioning Freud. After all, I had worked out my experiments long before I understood his work. But then I heard the voice of my second personality: "If you do a thing like that, as if you had no knowledge of Freud, it would be a piece of trickery. You cannot build your life upon a lie." With that, the question was settled. From then on, I became an open partisan of Freud and fought for him. (*Memories, Dreams, Reflections*)

Although Jung is describing a major crisis of integrity, he engagingly makes it sound as if it were a near thing. I doubt he got so near obeying "the devil's" circumspect suggestion as he modestly suggests. There are two qualities of playfulness in this serious passage—the adult like a child has made up a set of rules (Jung's "You cannot build your life upon a lie") and then deliberately chooses to obey the rules, just as in a game.

Most helpful to integrity (as to play) is the boundary of *time*—and specifically the boundary between this very moment and all the shimmering, unnerving *future*. Jung looked forward and did some cost-benefit thinking: my future will be threatened if I honor this unpopular Freud. Then he locked off the future by making up a rule, and he stayed inside that game long enough to give Freud the proper acknowledgments in his paper. Children, as do adults, lock off all time but the moment in order to be a decision-making personality like God. (I will be the mother and the street cleaner; you can be the priest and the DWI driver, etc.)

God, after all, makes up the rules and decides to bear with them or shove other people into bearing with them. To play at being a parent is to be like God for this moment. The reason such play leads later to integrity, I think, is that God doesn't do cheap things, so in adult life we play at being like him, and we try to have at least some moments in life when we aren't watching the main chance—being cheap. Everyone, as did Jung, has a look forward at the decision-making moment: "Yeah, I'd like to do that straight good thing but, if I do, where'll that get me?" The integrity-experiencing process then stops that moment, deliberately *walls off the future*, makes all time just this moment of time, so the person can do the difficult thing.

In these two examples, the one of playing dollhouse and the other of Jung practicing integrity, a common element has appeared: the playful aspect of making up rules and then either obeying or disobeying them. It is fun to make rules and set values. "This is good," "this is bad"; "we shall do this," "we shan't do that." When we decide to stay within the rules, we have invented, so to speak, a moral genie in the bottle. When we decide to ignore the rules, our moral instinct is dispersed like expanding air. The pleasure of obedience lasts somewhat longer than the pleasure of disobedience; for example, winning Monopoly by the rules is a slow-going thing—all those hours of acquiring property by luck or by connivance and such venal trading as one can pull off. Winning by cheating at the bank or by simply giving oneself the property cards wanted gives just about one minute's pleasure and then the most awful torpor sets in. Next, this torpor has the property of making one want to lie down before even picking up the board and all the mess. That is the passivity in question. After boundaries or rules are removed, torpor follows, and passivity a close second phase behind it. Because the passivity does not follow directly upon the rule breaking or rule ignoring, we have failed to identify its relationship to rule breaking—a second-phase result.

Nineteen forty is a useful approximate date for the removing of space boundaries from American domestic life. The younger generation owned cars then, and drove them around. That ended the family circle on Sunday, and widened the province of young people far beyond neighborhood or village. Then, 1950 serves as a kind of approximate date for the removal of time-sense boundaries: television removed the telling of the story which had a beginning and a time limit in it. There is not a television drama in the world that begins with "Once upon a time"—and almost symbolically you can hardly sell a television play today unless it is part of a series. In other words, the time container has been removed: most viewers can't concentrate quickly enough to enjoy a single episode. It must be torpidly ongoing. The soaps are built on a minimum of thirteen times. A mini is three times. Because there is no time limit (such as *once*—just once, not twice—upon a time there was a king, etc.) everything in the world becomes ongoing by implication. It is impossible to make up rules. You can't be designated the father, nor I the mother, and John the police, and this the house, because the psyche is nervously already expecting the next set of characters to come on and the scene will shift. We can't hold the picture long enough to give our hearts to it— playfully.

Making up rules, ethical ones for example, is one way of imposing order upon chaos (that old campsite-improvement instinct of our species). Animals may not bother with change of matériel; we are not happy unless we are plugging away at it.

Probably ethics are fun because they are a genuine inner form of campsite improvement. They are good fun somewhat in the way religion seemed to be fun for the Schoolmen; they were always seeing its characteristics as being symbolized by normal outer experiences. God had his chain of being, then, to which man's chain of being was simply analogous. Not an idea dear to the heart of the serfs at the very bottom of the lord's estate, but then no one asked their opinion. In any case, always the inner order was deliberately being imposed, and our everyday life became merely its symbols. It is a point of view that verges on being simply crazy. It invites scorn until one has a look at the alternative: what if the outer world, with such real-estate actions as we take, symbolizes nothing, and means nothing but itself? The first thing that happens is that we need study no particular part of it; it is a long meaningless skein. Therefore, we don't need to mark off this part *in time* and say, "Once long before Noah was born, long before your grandmother's grandmother could make fire, etc." and we don't need to mark off any part *in place* either, and say, "This will be the house, I will be the mother, John will be the baby." Nothing needs much study, and nothing needs to be held for a moment before the imagination so we can devote ourselves to it. It will all be ongoing.

Most adult consciousness is quite close to that now. Most thought is just recording the ongoing outer reality. Now, if that does not create cheating, torpor next, then passivity, and if it is fun, we might as well carry on without caviling. But if our culture seems to have quite a lot of cheating followed by torpor and in turn by passivity, we ought to try returning to the bottle and genie of ethics. Here is the problem—in ethics, all time is present time. Therefore, I will not think of the future (I will not think of what the others will say). I will think only of the problem. I will deliberately—like a child deciding the doll-house plot—decide to act in such and such a way.

# Our Class System

*Landmarks are disappearing rapidly. Why should I fret over the loss of a raw-boned farmhouse on a bleak hillside, or an obsolete schoolhouse back in a grove? Because they are cairns and buoys by which we circumnavigate the social landscape. Without them we will never know where we are—or who.*

—Newell Searle, Assistant Director,
Minnesota Humanities Commission

Once I was lost in Paris. I had got away from the Seine, on the Left Bank, and eventually came to the Place de Saint Sulpice, named for the church in its center. All round the square were small and large shops selling devotional statuary—not hundreds but thousands of plasticine Virgins and Josephs and Marys, donkeys visiting Christ, the sheep and the Wise Men, shepherds. Those I handled were white, ready to be painted by the buyer or perhaps to be left white for the effect of purity. I saw little attempt by the sculptors to *start where the people are*— that convincing approach of grantsmen and teachers.

These figures started, rather, in some dreamhouse of Western religions. Animals, men, son of God—all were refined, all pure white; the people had the high foreheads of Norman and Breton Frenchmen. There was no nonsense about the Wise Men's having had to ride camels or sleep several nights in these robes. These camels did not bite, and unlike Eliot's, were not refractory. As I looked at the thousands of figures (for there were several shop windows full of them), I realized that the villages the Wise Men passed through were full of latent theologians and apparently we who buy figures for our crêches are latent theologians, too—even those of us who buy the worst offenders, the tiny Veronicas with bloody veils and the youths that look like Shattuck boys with daubs of red spots on palms and feet, or the Virgins for some reason placed in tiny Coldstream sentry boxes. Parisians call all such devotional crockery *saint sulpice,* since so much of it is sold around that church.

What is the good of *saint sulpice?* The good of it is that whoever thought up the idea of a crêche at all, who was likely St. Francis of Assisi, had heart to know that *starting where the people are* is at best useless. What we all care for is what we yearn to be—not what or where we seem to be. Any art, even *saint sulpice,* that reminds us of what we yearn to be is a help.

I was reminded of the little religious statues one weekend in March of this past year. I had driven across southern Minnesota to give a talk. Like other speakers, I rehearsed in the car. I gave my talk to the steering wheel (aloud) and made up the questions and fielded them, answering those I could, asking for help from the imaginary audience for those I couldn't. At three o'clock in the afternoon I checked into the motel room reserved for me, and went over the whole talk again. At seven I went and gave the talk. It wasn't much good.

There are so many ways to give an indifferent talk despite all one's efforts! In any event, I had that experience. It is embarrassing to do a dumb job of something and be paid generously for it and have it received kindly. I didn't sleep very well that night. The man in the room next to mine was pretty sick most of the night. He thumped around his room a lot, and sometimes he was sick at one end of it, and sometimes at the other. He did not quiet down until three o'clock in the morning. At six I got up and left.

As I was turning the key in my car door, I saw there was the most wonderful March frost all over everything. It was very slight. It lay slick and lacy on the motel turn-around and on Minnesota 19. Its fragile tails lay along the oak branches. In the rear side window of my car I saw my reflection and I looked all right: no one could see that this person had taken pay for a dull speech and then hadn't slept very well.

Just then the man from next door came out to start his car. He too looked all right—groomed and brisk. He looked a little formalized, the way the ill do when they have sluiced their faces and mean to keep their troubles to themselves. He even looked like an ad for our species: Reliable Human Being with Sensibility, Moral Substance, Experienced in Idealistic Projects: Inquire Within. No one could guess he had been sick all over his motel room all night and had infuriated his neighbor and possibly did for a living nothing more numinous than designing comic-strip layouts for appliance retailers. He and I both looked very nice, and as I drove away in the cold, fine morning, Minnesota looked wonderful.

I drove a long time before stopping for breakfast because for some reason I got to thinking of those unimpressive little crèche figures I'd once seen in Paris. The image of them kept coming to mind. At last I understood that the whited look of Blue Earth County must have done it—or the idealized look which two tired, not very successful human beings had managed to achieve. So it struck me: no matter how mediocre people's recent record, they still wish to recognize the part of themselves that is like the stiff little crèche figures—the part that is astir with symbol.

It follows that when the symbolic past is destroyed in our landscape it is not just the sensitive who lose by it: we all do. We had better know that hungover salesmen and mediocre speakers have very good dreams of humanity in them—everybody must have—and therefore the gradual takeover of corrugated bins, alas so much cheaper and faster to put up than our 1940s barns, and the takeover of highway sprawl, and the heartless pushing over and burning of farmstead groves are damaging to the inner life not just of conscious Minnesotans like Newell Searle of the Humanities Commission, who see landscape as buoys marking things far under the surface, but to everyone.

Unfortunately people who work hard at saving the Minnesota landscape tend to think they are saving its beauty for themselves and for others equally sensitive to beauty. Beyond that, in their view of things, lie the coarse masses who drop the gum wrappers into Minnetonka and the Brule. In their view, there are the very few hard-pressed good guys losing the landscape to a plethora of bad guys. Their view is a luxury. To save the past and present beauty of Minnesota we shall have to give up that very view, which Americans hold dear. We shall have to give up our kind of class system.

I do not mean our social class system, through which one can wander however one likes, upward or downward. Anyone can gradually learn to call women women instead of ladies, or to polish bare wood instead of laying broadloom, or to call one's people parents instead of folks—or do whatever's wanted. All those class markings are no problem to anyone; what is serious is that underneath all that, and underneath our pointing at British snobbery, we have a strongbox class lockup that I find disgusting. Its basic premise is: some people have an ethical or an aesthetic nature and others simply haven't. It is a lie, a lie which sits at table right next to a truth which is that some people are conscious of their ethical or aesthetic nature; others are unconscious of it. But everybody has it.

For everyone fretting aloud over the loss of "a raw-boned farmhouse on a bleak hillside" there are others who experience the same deprivation but so unconsciously that it shows only as undifferentiated despondency. Even the smiling drinker, easing himself heavily between boothback and table in the VFW lounge, is offended and frightened by the wrecking of the Minnesota landscape. He is offended, that is, with that fraction of his daily conscious thought not already absorbed by response to financial squeeze. He perceives wreckage of fishing lakes as an enemy, all right, but this enemy is only 3 percent (or so) of the total host lined up against him: the nearest enemy soldiery are economic pressure, boredom, lack of leisure, daily discourtesies given and received simply because no one taught an alternative to them.

Let's imagine a soldier dug in on Anzio beachhead, with the German emplacements very close and very high above the American positions, and then tell that soldier that four kilometers behind the high ground some boys have laid two-by-fours across the road with twenty-penny nails sticking up along them, so that when the U.S. supply trucks try to advance they will get flats. Then if you ask the soldier, "Do you feel threatened by those little boys? They are your natural enemy, you know!" the soldier can't take you seriously: visible before him are all those gray helmets. It is something the same with the VFW drinker. If he appears not to be taking up for conservation of the woods, it is not necessarily that he is insensitive to beauty. He scarcely has time, he is so pressed upon by other things. It is a psychological parallel to a soldier's already having to point a rifle in too many directions.

Further, natural beauty is a low priority with nearly all of us. We may grieve for the vanishing past or despoiled present beauty; we may acknowledge that reminders—like well-loved farm sites—incline us to spirit, but we can only occasionally be roused on the subject; whether taught it in the VFW or the Episcopal church or the Countryside Council, the fact is we have been taught that economic reality is important, and psychic reality is at its best a luxury consideration, and at its usual worst, slaver.

Of course Minnesotans will continue staging fights to preserve our landscape—and not just those showing up at Spring Hill conferences called Partners for a Livable Minnesota, but Minnesotans by the hundreds. Their efforts will be useful only if they abandon the notion that some people don't need symbol and beauty. When a class system operates in the *psyche* then it has arrived at full depravity. Surely the worst use of *saint sulpice* is preferable to deciding out of hand that some people haven't holy insides and holy needs.

# Chin Up in a Rotting Culture

I am going to propose a way for rural Minnesota to participate in our rotting national culture.

Minnesota country life is more agreeable than most twentieth-century American life of late; Minnesota itself is still more beautiful than most places where Americans have to live. So we don't write many letters to Congressmen. When the priest asks us to pray for those in agony in Nicaragua and Rhodesia and to pray for the Whole State of Christ's Church I notice we all look a little vague. We do not participate actively in the general rot or in the general pain.

But it participates in us. Sadness from its sadness has been flung into our hearts even if we are only spasmodically conscious of it. This sadness is in our unconscious hearts, even here where we walk in the October basswoods and emerge on the lake's harsh edge, where everything ventures to say: the world is absolutely lovely! it is absolutely lovely—what else?

No need to complain where complaint isn't due. Indeed, the surface life of America, if you've any sort of financial security, is marvelous. It is plainly fun. By the millions, we get to drive around in strong cars, wherever we like—although we are running out of fuel. We visit and live in heated places although we are running out of fuel; we hear cellists from countries in sore pain under communism. We pig up joyfully on food imported from countries wrecking the dollar. And nearly everyone gets to go nearly everywhere: Freddy Laker is going to haul people over to London's Stanstead and Gatwick Airports who twenty years ago would have considered Kansas City, as in the musical, "about as far as a person oughta go."

At certain points in decay most cultures do offer pleasure in the surface life. The Merovingians' judicial system was such that people opted for death rather than their idea of *habeas corpus*—yet the populace lived generally well. On the eve of the Turkish takeover, relatives of crusaders and relatives of Constantine XIII enjoyed profitable investments.

Now, it isn't true that Americans, or Minnesotans, are lying around like the later Romans, being handed around grapes by *famuli bene dependeti*—but it is nearly true. I allow myself hours and hours every day in which not to think about the creeping rot in our culture. Whole days, too. In truth, months go by when I don't. Others must be doing the same. The surface of American life is variegated and genial.

If the part of life acknowledged by conscious thought and feeling is both genial and amusing, then why stir up grief? In law, of course, grief must be stirred up. If egg shampoos are found not to have eggs they must be recalled. When our principal intelligence service is found to have imprisoned a man alone in a concrete room for three years, he must be released and Americans must be informed as the Minneapolis *Tribune* did on September 16, 1978. The question is not will we correct social evils, because of course we will, and rotting culture or no, we still have dozens of agencies both inside and outside the government devoted to doing so. Americans are still terrific at exposing and punishing violations of public trust. The question here is why should anyone try to remain *conscious* of our rotting culture from day to day?

Each year the Chambers of Commerce in Minnesota towns plan their activities. In my town, Madison, the area Chamber duly convened its publicity committee for 1978. The publicity committee had drawings of a thirty-six- to forty-foot-long lutefisk (lye-drenched codfish—a Norwegian *Vestlandets specialitet*), to be about six feet high of aluminum tubing and green-gold cloth stretched about. Five guys, the chairman explained, would walk along inside the lutefisk at parades in Madison and neighboring towns. (This would show the flag a little: Madison, Minnesota, consumes more lutefisk per capita than any city in the world except Bergen.) After a lot of delay I got my part of the job done—handing in an estimate of square yardage of cloth needed for fish skin and fins. Then the publicity committee never met again and, so far as I know, never built the lutefisk. This in a town which in years past has put on entire melodramas directed by Lutheran intern clergymen, written by high school faculty members. One year the baker baked two hundred cookies to make the tiled roof of the witch's house for a street production of Hansel and Gretel, and refused any payment. The Catholic priest bought the gingerbread house at auction, and for years, St. Michael's School first graders got to play in it after Reading. So why did nothing come of the lutefisk and of much else we have planned recently?

There are the usual explanations why things don't get done—inflation, for one. But under these lies a sharper reason, which interests me here. The conscious mind of Minnesota small towns has always shouted: Our life is still all right! We do not have to live in impersonal cities. We still have fun together—look at the county fair. Our teenagers are not destructive. These remarks presuppose the old Midwest genius for locking out the outside world and being good and worthy by ourselves. The unconscious, however, is always inviting in information from beyond town walls, and beyond the fields: it drinks up everything offered by television and news heads. However hastily a skilled isolationist turns the pages of the Minneapolis *Tribune*, the unconscious, with its speed of light, picks up all the awful news and hurries back down inside ourselves with it, like a dwarf hiding a treasure of poison. What is carried down there, and which we must carry about inside us, is grief over our rotting culture. It gives us just enough general malaise so we don't get around to building forty-foot lutefisk floats.

I would like to list four examples of national-level rot which are all known about but too seldom consciously considered by rural Minnesotans:

| *Example* | *Meaning* |
|---|---|
| 1. Egg shampoos without eggs | 1. Willingness to cheat others for profit |
| 2. Trebling of advertising by firms discovered to be producing toxic or radioactive items | 2. Willingness to hurt or kill for profit |
| 3. Excessive numbers of academic talk conferences in elegant surroundings, grant-supported, on major moral issues | 3. Willingness to do psychological displacement of anxiety, at public expense, for the geniality of it |
| 4. The fate of Yuri Nosenke | 4. Willingness to torture a foreigner for three years, our opinion of Nazi and Soviet methods notwithstanding |

The above four examples, standing for dozens more like them, lie in the unconscious of the most robust and thickheaded local boosters.

Yet some towns—most engagingly, perhaps, Olivia, Minnesota—are actually increasing their voluntary recreational life together. They most succeed when they are not trying to play while Rome burns, but rather trying to be serious together. Olivia brought in two poets-in-residence, Nancy and Joe Paddock. Nancy and Joe never gave them a lovely poem about quilt making or the land or birds without adding the swift cry, though all this is lovely, it needs an ethic! Everything needs an ethic! So they worked to do what Chamber publicity committees work *not* to do: they worked to fasten together conscious and unconscious morality.

Small-town conscious morality involves fair and permanent

sexual patterning, fair and generous work for the day's wage, and generous serving of one another at death and during pain. Those are conscious. We like talking about how well we perform them, too.

I would like to propose that small-town Minnesota participate in our national griefs in the following way. I propose that the city council or the Chamber or some major group meet every Feast of St. Nicholas (December 6) and decide upon five or six figures who have done marvelous service to the American people at large. Any date for this would do. I commend St. Nicholas's Feast because he was patron saint of just about everybody, especially people of disparate social station, such as pawnbrokers and of course children, and his feast is at the end of the year, a logical time.

In 1962, Dr. Frances Kelsey, a medical officer of the FDA, received the President's Award for Distinguished Federal Civilian Service because she refused to let two companies, Merrill and National Drug, market thalidomide in this country. Dr. Kelsey received thanks from her own community, and many thanks from individual people, but no citations from towns in the United States, community groups as such. None, although we all saw the photographs of the children whose mothers had taken the drug made in Ansbach-an-See. It would have been marvelous if ten thousand city councils in America—or churches, even (churches! where were they?)—had written to Dr. Kelsey and said:

> Of course this is hopelessly inadequate but we are grateful for your action so we are sending you this plaque [quilt, mittens, hand-italic-printed copy of St. Matthew's Gospel with decorations swiped from Dürer's woodcuts]. (Or if the town or group is rich it could send an encyclopedia of world art with really good plates in it, or season tickets to the Arena Theatre: Dr. Kelsey lives in Kenwood, Maryland—she might like that.)

I want to add quickly that this would not mean much to Dr. Kelsey. In late September this year I talked to her on the phone. I was breathless with admiration left over from 1962. I cannot describe how indifferent she was to my chattering praise or to the proposal I make here. Apparently you cannot change unegotistical people: if they don't learn to crave flattery when they are young, they don't develop a taste for it later.

The value in the deliberate, yearly praise of public figures would lie in enabling rural people to participate in morality, not just locally at the fair stand, but nationally, and to relate to serious issues. Killing and maiming people is something we must think about. As Marianne Moore wrote:

> quiet form upon the dust, I cannot
> look and yet I must.

Finally, there will be a lovely side effect if we do it: it means once a year we argue about very good people. We won't agree on who should get our praise. We will lose sight of how unimportant our praise is; we will lose sight of ourselves a bit. We will be thinking about national-scale virtues.

We could do some condemnations, too. I like a fight.

# A Mongoose Is Missing

[The cobra] spread out his hood more than ever, and Rikki-tikki
saw the spectacle-mark on the back of it that looks exactly like
the eye part of a hook-and-eye fastening. He was afraid for the
minute; but it is impossible for a mongoose to stay frightened
for any length of time, and though Rikki-tikki had never met a
live cobra before, his mother had fed him on dead ones, and he
knew that all a grown mongoose's business in life was was to
fight and eat snakes. . . .

Rikki-tikki had a right to be proud of himself; but he did not
grow too proud, and he kept that garden as a mongoose should
keep it, with tooth and jump and spring and bite, till never a cobra dared show its head inside the walls.
—Rudyard Kipling, "Rikki-Tikki-Tavi"

At last there is a way in which unsophisticated country people
are *less* repressed than sophisticated urban people. For over a
decade it has been axiomatic that educated urban elements
have learned to face their feelings better than small-town people; they use available psychotherapeutic services with élan;
they belong to Group, not American Lutheran Church Wom-
en's Circle; they know the right things to say—such as *we* are
not always right and *they* always wrong. Their conversations

are jeweled with smooth stones like "You know, when you're that angry at someone, it's usually that very thing inside yourself that you're *really* angry at." They know all about projection and association, and usually have a little repertoire of stories illustrating a colleague's lack of individuation. Yet there is one form of major repression of the 1970s to which psychological sophisticates are more subject than are Minnesota rural people: it is repression of the ancient, infinitely practical instinct to isolate ignobility from the community.

Nobility itself is a little out of style, like Kipling and more recently Hemingway, who dreamed about it. Humankind is a partisan, right-and-wrong-thinking race, so we don't just peaceably let something slip out of style: we stomp it on its way. Bloomsbury finished off Kipling ages ago with "O dear, straight British Empire, best beloved!" and similar sarcasm. Our helping professions have developed and proliferated a special set of pejorative language just for people who try to identify ignobility and then pay attention to it: The best-known words of this language are *judgmental, rigid* (or *inflexible*), and *punitive.*

In my town, at least, we are still judgmental, rigid, and punitive about bad behavior. We still do the classic American small-town process of slightly isolating anyone who is practicing selfishness at others' expense. We don't ostracize them (we haven't that luxury—sooner or later we shall have to do daily business with them: sell them things, help their kids learn lay-ups, let them fill our teeth, as the case may be); we don't exactly drop them. We see them less.

To a therapy-oriented world this sounds provincial indeed. In fact, it is practical. Immorality is something of a contagion. If cheats and liars associate freely with those trying at some cost to themselves *not* to cheat and lie, the simple result is that the latter won't try so hard in future. Any school headmaster knows enough to write home if someone's son or daughter "is keeping undesirable company." We edge away, in our towns, we do not keep company, with people committing embezzlement, adultery, and crooked figuring of hours spent in repair work.

We edge away from a plumber who tells Mrs. Hofstad, "I have to go back to town to get a part for that," and then takes the pickup over to Mrs. Beske's house, puts in a half hour there, and then explains to her, "We're going to have to get a gasket for that," then returns to Mrs. Hofstad's, and subsequently charges both women for all the time involved. We spread the word about such behavior in a rigid, judging, and punitive way: that kind of behavior is bad.

If moral division is natural to our species at this era of our evolution, then we not only need to do it, but we simply will do it. When we do it well, it will be our genius for discernment; when we do it poorly, we will be wrong-headed and name callers—but for better or worse that faculty is at work. If psychological fashion declares dividing of good from bad to be archaic, we are likely to be daunted and to try to repress the instinct. After all, the psychological community are daunting to most of us: they are better-dressed and more authoritative and they know our sexual secrets and God knows what all else besides. They have offices with true slimers outside the doors who say things like "Doctor will see you now." If we have anything of the social climber in us we are likely to believe them when they say right and wrong are archaic concepts; we too may start using expressions like "irresponsible" instead of "cruel" or "crooked." We may repress right and wrong. So down into the unconscious it goes. And, to the parent who had abandoned his or her five children in favor of a fulfilling midlife crisis, we smile cordially and ask, "Are you coping? Are you all right?"

If the instinct to judge and isolate has gone down into the unconscious, where will it show up? It is useful to define *isolating*. To isolate someone is to refuse to participate in his destiny, and to refuse to take his needs to heart. Then the questions to ask are: Whose destiny do Americans tend to refuse to participate in? And whose needs do we proverbially fail to take to heart?

We are a money-making culture, with a minor in recreational sex—to put us in our worst light. People who do not make money and who do not practice recreational sex include children, the aged, and the dying. Those whose destiny we do not participate in enough are children, the aged, and the dying. We are famous, in everyone's sociology, for not taking their needs to heart—but there is something worse about it: not only do we not take their needs to heart, but we practice behavior modification on all three groups. They are the subjects of our experimentation. However harmless the experimentation, being a subject is still being a subject. It is as if the coarsest kind of vengeance were working itself out in our unconscious: The children, the old, the dying fail us as colleagues in money-making and recreational sex; we retaliate by making them lab subjects, not human beings.

Sometimes this unconscious hostility is practiced only as negligence of their best interests. For example, as a society we have done very little to cut down children's television-watching, although an appalling relationship has been established between TV and dyslexia in male children. TV (as opposed to film screen) disallows a certain normal eye-muscle response, so a child watching a lot of TV is engaging for the first time in physiological history in stationing the eye. A result is dyslexia. Two very recent reports which point out our responsibility in this new crisis are *The TV Report* by Robert W. Morse, Regional Religious Educational Coordinators of the Episcopal Church, 815 Second Avenue, New York, N.Y. 10007; and Marshall McLuhan's speech on KSJN (Minnesota Public Radio), November 18, 1978, available on cassette from Minnesota Public Radio, 400 Sibley Street, St. Paul, Minnesota 55101. Only unconscious hostility, in this case idly landing on the children, explains why we allow TV watching to continue in homes where there are small children. Indeed, we have brought TV into our schools.

I think we would be on a kinder course if we criticized openly those who threaten us. The 1960s produced a new permissive attitude toward crimes of all kinds, and it produced the most disturbing trend in children's books in a long time. A new genre of children's picture book appeared, in which death was the subject, and the drawings were large and spooky, and in the end the protagonist died with a lot of affected psychoslime attached. In one book, the man gave away his heart and his mind and his other vital parts until he was all given away. It seemed like such a touching book, so sensitive, so marvelously taking children at their intuitive, able-to-cope-with-seriousthings level—until you finished reading it and realized it was simply trendy sadism. The children listening directly experienced the horrors, in aid of nothing in particular. These books all had minimal plots, and a spacy sort of Marin County Weltanschauung about them. How very different their "sensitivity" is from the pure, straight affection of Kipling's calling his readers Best Beloved on the one hand and killing off both cobras, without any nonsense. It is an act of hostility to pretend to tell a story and then not supply a plot. It takes energy, though, to write a plot for children. Perhaps Kipling's yarn about Rikki-tikki-tavi is so thoroughgoing a story because the author didn't waste energy suppressing a natural dislike of cobras. He didn't tell himself that cobras need understanding, perhaps therapy, even. E. B. White—also a generous plotter, whose psychology has no slickness—never suggests to children that Templeton the rat is "fulfilling himself." He suggests to children that Templeton the rat has a revolting, abysmally selfish personality and never does anything decent unless bribed to the barn roof. The great children's writers, such as Kipling, Rumer Godden, E. Nesbit, E. B. White, and Ted

Hughes, know for one thing that an open battle between good and bad is the birthplace of humor.

It takes energy to suppress a natural dislike of adultery and robbery, avarice and treachery. All this open-mindedness! And such strictures it lays on us: you must hate the sin, but love the sinner! That particular piece of medieval Christianity has been very strangely resurrected by current psychology; it is tottering about like something from a Regensburg lab in the horror movies. Whoever heard of hating snakebite and loving cobras?

If we continue to suppress judgment, rigidity, and punitiveness, wrongdoing will thunder closer and closer to the center of civilization. Then there will be rage about it; more books will be written about lying in high places, surprising corruptions, amazing treachery unsuspected for decades, and if society itself can be said to feel self-hatred it will feel it more and more, but it will be an ever more unconscious sort of shimmering, unclear hatred, hard to identify. And in this thunder of greed and fear, the children, the sick, and the old will fly off into something like total psychic isolation, like people flung out into space at night. Since good and bad will be out of style, we will fail children by not reading them literature about courageous mongooses. In fact, we are already failing our children that way.

# To Be Rude and Hopeful
# Instead of
# Whining and Quitting

The two most prominent activities of the countryside, farming and community, are so disheartening now that it is tempting to whine and quit. In fact, whining and quitting are increasing.

The causes for the failures in Minnesota family farming are very different from the causes for the failures in Minnesota community life: most important, the farms are collapsing from the external pressures of our economy, not merely from sloth or local apathy. It is convenient for the USDA, for realty interests, and for related brokerage houses to convert the Middle West from middle-sized farms to large corporate farms, from large corporate farms to larger ones, to subdivisions, etc. Stewardship of the land declines in such a progression; pride and versatility disappear from the daily life of the cash-renter farmer—but never mind, the land has entered the American cash economy.

It is grievous to hear family-farm operators saying, "If only those Ag Land Fund people out there or the government or whoever it is back East just would come out here, they'd understand our needs, and they'd help us devise programs to save the family farm." It is grievous to hear that because of the disheartening naïveté of it. Those "people back East" and "those people in Washington" already understand the family farmers' needs. They simply are on the other side. Their long-range investment aims presuppose the family farmer's failure.

Minnesota farmers can just barely imagine that someone somewhere else actually *wants* them run off their land. People they will never meet at Kiwanis have devised tax write-offs for machinery acquisition that are designed deliberately to give the large operators a leg up. I expect the reason the farmer finds it difficult to believe this is that, unless he has received Farmers Union or equivalent training, he probably knows little about economics, so he is not even acquainted with the notion of the impersonal force of economic development. North Dakota farmers experienced and resisted that force in the late nineteenth century, but most Minnesota farmers are still ignorant of the fight their neighbors put up. Most Minnesota farmers live as if the battles against the railroads, for example, had never taken place. They live outside their own history.

Secondly, every single person whom a Minnesota farmer meets socially desires his well-being. The Coast-to-Coast man is for him. If it is dry, everybody from the clerks at the Ben Franklin store to the owner of the Chevy garage assures him that we sure could use some "moisture," which is even his word. By the time a farmer is fifty he has spent well over thirty years receiving incidental backup from all those miscellaneous conversations on Main Street or leaning against the fairstand flaps or sitting at the Bingo table in the narthex. Not once has anyone pointed out, "I will be better off when you go under." Townspeople get cross at the farmers for constantly grousing, but it is only the grousing that annoys them: they don't doubt his value as an economic entity.

I go into all this in order to show something interesting about whining and quitting. Whining is an appropriate reaction to stress *when you don't know how to fight back*. It befits small farmers, therefore, just as it befits draftees. But whining does *not* befit people working in community organization. They can perfectly well improve their lot. No gigantic Keynesian or Smithian forces are casting them aside. If they are whining and quitting, they do it from accidie; they do it instead of reforming.

Some emotional responses are a contagion, on two levels. If everyone around us has them, we catch them, and secondarily, once they have entered our personality they infect everything else there. Rural townspeople catch whining and quitting from the disheartened farmers. Then, once inside the town dweller, like social climbing or gambling, it begins to eat up his other emotional life. We all know the classic syndrome of gambling: the love of the odds wolfs down all of one's other interests and responsibilities. The inveterate gambler cares ever less for home or hearth or travel or love or his eventual death: only the stake shimmers in his mind's eye. That is *in extremis*. In the moderate range, social climbing and whining-and-quitting eat up our daily enthusiasm about things, the cheerful gifts of the imagination, such as that funny slight sexual feeling one has in the morning opening the door to the tomcat returned with one ear frankly chewed through, the other totally missing, one eye swollen shut, the left rear leg being carried with what luckily looks like simple fracturing; but Tom has lustrously washed the other three paws although it is not yet seven o'clock, and his carriage says this isn't the last time this will happen, it was worth it, we just ought to see the other fellow. Whiners-and-quitters, like social climbers, merely have the cat fixed.

If we are to save small-town community life, surrounded as we are by the dying American family farm, we shall have to weigh everything working against us. The 1960s worked against us psychologically. It introduced a generation who were convinced that organizational talent threatened sensual fulfillment. The *cri de décade* was: We must get back to our natural life!—as if political organization were unnatural to mankind. In an article in *Spring*, a discursive magazine of psychology and philosophy, the psychoanalyst Mary Ann Mattoon observes that politics are a natural part of the human personality, and that therefore, we must exercise that part of us or it will atrophy and turn to poison. But the 1960s style was to ignore that part of us. Kenneth Rexroth, who was always prompt to cut through any sentimental view of America's "greening," made a memorable sour-headed remark about communes. "Don't talk to me about communes!" he shouted in 1968—early days, then. "All they are is dozens of otherwise intelligent women baking bread all day!" Between 1968 and 1970 I met something like one hundred women living in Marin County communes and they were all angry. They all claimed to be "finding their true selves" but anger lighted their eyes and wrists. They were being shrunk and poisoned by political atrophy.

I bring it up here because those people are now over thirty: they and their movement have filtered back from San Francisco even to rural Minnesota. Their laid-back philosophy has entered our community life.

So we have at least these two psychological forces working against small-town life: the apprehensive feelings of the farmers, which magnetize our feelings, and second, the 1960s apathy to organization.

Humanity has three talents that at their best are rather romantic: the talent of memory used to good purpose, the talent of being convinced that we have some profound task to do in this universe, and the talent of inventing social structures. The talent of memory makes us poets, philosophers, and historians—and when it goes rotten, it becomes the neurotic's exercise of playing over and over the same scenes, bent. The talent of belief that our species has some special destined duty makes us a religious animal (which we are, like it or no). We look to the future when we are inspired, not to the past. At its best, this talent makes us feel oddly *beckoned* forward. Its shadow side is sentimental apprehension, which Burns exemplifies in his remark to the fieldmouse: "Still thou art blest, compar'd wi' me! The present only toucheth thee: But, och! I backward cast my e'e on prospects drear! An' forward tho' I canna see, I guess an' fear!"

The third talent is for inventing social structures. In celebratory things we call these structures *community;* in regulatory things, we call them *government.* When this talent goes slack, we find ourselves yawning between the bylaws and among the nine-by-seventeen pans of bars. Slipshod community is the more noticeable in rural Minnesota, where the other two gifts—the life of memory and life of religion—are so much subordinated to it.

A look round usually confirms suspicions that neither Ardyce Lutheran Church nor St. Swithin's in the Swamp (and even less any civic group) is serving the following very well: the poor, the old, the alcoholics and other drug dependents, the divorced, and all single people between the ages of nineteen and ninety. If these people attend regularly they therefore get all the boredom and nothing in ego return. The other people (those with enough money, those capable of leadership, those bringing up school-age children—the backbone of the community) get the same boredom, but it is diluted with peer-group acceptance, and nearly every sermon, what's more, is focused on them. They feel at least visible. This is partly because nearly every clergyman thinks that if he weren't a clergyman he would be in business or in another profession; he does not imagine that if he weren't a clergyman he might be a drunk, an indigent, or a cuckold. His moralizing sermons are naturally directed to those he identifies with, who have power over their own circumstances. If something like 85 percent of the sermons given in rural American churches are against materialism, those sermons are directed at people who have the choice of being materialistic or not. No one admonishes someone for being materialistic who has a wringer washer on the porch and sheep grazing right up to the house. (Sheep grazing right up to the house, by the way, is the classic instance of rural poverty. It is the rural equivalent of drying your clothes on a relay line between the fourth floor of your building and the fourth floor of the building opposite, in New York.)

I chose churches as examples of community life because they are still the major structure in Minnesota towns. Actually, there are no other groups in town that do any better with the poor, the old, the single, etc. Our town organizations are far too slipshod for our needs. The situation can be corrected, I think, and what's more, it can be corrected without very much imagination or expenditure of energy.

If every person concerned would make a list of ten goals he or she would like to see accomplished by a small-town *structure* of any kind—any civic group, private club, any organization or church—and then make another list of those structures that exist in the community, we could then shuffle goals and groups and arrive at different job descriptions. It is not a new idea. The Farmers Union, with the National Endowment for the Humanities, has a program for bringing ethical, historical, and literary considerations to its members.

Theoretically, the nineteenth-century town hall brought decision making to farmers. But it didn't. Then, in the twentieth century, again theoretically, the schools brought the humanities into rural life—but they really didn't do it. So why shouldn't the Farmers Union have a go at it? I think this whole idea of shaking up jobs is very hopeful. It means we can stop whining and being alienated by such-and-such a structure and simply say, "That group is apparently failing one hundred percent at the job assigned. Let's assign them another one!" It does mean making a list. I would like to offer the one on page 157.

In any event, these are rough ideas whose only virtue may

be that they enable us to regard present failures without giving up. We must not abdicate from that engaging genius we have for gathering ourselves to do things together. I don't think abdication ever works; the moment we left the throne, the throne jumped into our hearts. There it sits heavily. No matter how we stare at the polo ponies from the ivory table of drinks, nothing is interesting except that throne. And those who leave Kiwanis in anger do not relax in the noonday shade the way lions do. Apparently we haven't the lion's choice. Apparently we must go back to Kiwanis and say, "The church has failed to gather all the senior citizens in the area (who would like to) into choosing a major work of art, such as Rembrandt or Constable or Cropsey, and projecting it onto a wall of the City Hall or outside along the side of the well drillers' building, and then working on it all summer, and asking some high school kid to write up something about it to be printed on the wall face below: shall we take it on or no?"

| Organization | What it is failing at | What we could assign it to see if it mightn't do refreshingly well at it | Which other group could do this group's present job better |
| --- | --- | --- | --- |
| St. Marvin's-on-the-Hill | Teaching morals, preserving symbols | Running problem-solving and therapy seminars | Farm organizations, with humanities grants |
| Weekly news-papers | Tough, genuine inquiry into community problems | Feature stories that would raise the rural self-image, and teach farmers economic and political history | Church newsletters (which have little to lose) |
| Women's circles, homemakers | Giving their members any serious, challenging purpose in family life | Zoning studies for keeping and increasing windbreaks, green belts, and other ways of preserving the countryside | Health-store proprietors—whose consumer philosophy is more responsible than women's present sources |

# Koko and Wolfgang Amadeus in Rural Minnesota

My town, Madison, did very well by a boy and man named Koko, who lived among us until his mama died and there was no one to care for him. No children cast jeers or ugly smiles at him that I ever saw; no one gingerly feeling his way home from the VFW lounge caught sight of Koko and projected a magma of angers onto him. Koko moved about freely, going to the movies, edging in and out of Lindrud's Ten Cents Store and Lund's Produce. He picked up old copies of our weekly paper here and there and we bought them from him. He placed the high school and band chairs in the park for the summer concerts. Especially he went to the movies. Usually not swift, Koko drew as fast as John Wayne: his index fingers came fast out of belt or pockets and he'd cry aloud in the movie house, "Yippee! Yippee! Kill 'im, you guys, kill that guy!" We didn't always choose to sit alongside Koko but then no one ever told him to shut up either, the way we did the little boys up front. And all day people said, "Hiya, Koko" on Sixth Avenue, our main street. He'd always answer and grin except when he was standing under the marquee, studying the stills of next week's Western: then Koko's eyes were already as round and blank as the sky that covers Stewart or Palance and all the Apaches that ever were.

We don't do nearly so well by the gifted or intellectual individual in our midst. If we imagine a Twin Cities person with enough inner resources or private library or tubes of paint so he or she can work in a rural setting—say, someone named Wolfgang Amadeus Emily Dickinson Orwell—we can see the logic in his spending a good deal of his time alone. After all, he left the congenial conversations of Twin Cities gathering places like The Restoration and Rusoff's Bookstore in order to concentrate. He won't want simply to substitute for those conversations, hour for hour, ours out here:

> After all those telephone calls you'd think it was perfectly clear or maybe it's just me, but Vern and Cheryl were going to bring the angelfood and LaVonne and Ardyce were supposed to bring the Wilderness cherry pie filling and then her and me were supposed to bring the Cool Whip, what does she do though but turn up with another can of Wilderness cherry pie filling and no Cool Whip so somebody had to go back to town and get some, well I said no way was I going back with no spare in the back of the pickup because DeWayne said first thing this morning he'd change that spare. You know DeWayne, though.

As soon as Wolfgang gets to the countryside two changes take place inside him: he realizes he will be bored and therefore he feels deserving of a bit of gratitude—after all, he is some sort of a blessing to the town, isn't he? He will pointedly go about becoming a blessing to the town. He will write a suite for the hundredth anniversary of the church, waving away all thanks; he will paint a large panel for the city hall; he will speak, between the Gettysburg Address and Taps, on Memorial Day. From time to time he will be in the weekly paper with the HR bill number family farmers probably ought to write their Congressmen about and remind them of the House zip code. He will always come from his strong side—his talent—whatever it is. He will give us tidbits of his major force—his field of endeavor. Because of the Wilderness-cherry-pie-filling conversations he will not really take the local people as his peers, and therefore he will ask them to change his freeze-pipe wrappings and meet him at Minneapolis/St. Paul International Airport but he won't hike over to the neighbors' to help them rassle three cars out of the ditch with tractors and chains, and he doesn't expect to be called and asked for a ride to the Zephyr bus stop.

He stops examining his own selfishness carefully, too, for the simple reason that human beings, no matter how noble, do stop examining their own selfishness when they aren't accosted daily by peers. One gets trial and clearance by peers, not by non-peers. The gifted Wolfgang in the countryside will soon start perceiving his selfishness as quite complicated psychic positions, fairly interesting. When someone calls and says we have twenty people making up a pan each of 1 pound beef roasted, then ground, 1 pound roast pork, ground, 1 tablespoon mayonnaise, 3 boiled eggs, ground in, 1 tablespoon Worcestershire sauce, then drain the fat from the meat juices, then put the clear juice back in, and stir, so we can spread buns with it for the funeral, our Wolfgang smiles ruefully because he would love more than anything to take part in these simple activities: no one knows better than he that this is the very stuff of country life, but he has huger work to do in his short life, longer hours to work in a day, greater responsibilities to his lifework than he could ever explain to those people! Coriolanus did not want to wear the wolf outfit for better reasons.

In time, Wolfgang will begin to feel extra-worthy, just for not living in St. Paul or Minneapolis among his peers. That is ominous but it is followed with the second inner change, which is worse: he will develop an odd greed for local admiration—as if it were deserved because, hero that Wolfgang is, he has so few congenial friends about him. It's fifty miles to the next painter, theologian, or musician. An odd fact of human nature is that people merely *want* their proper food but literally *crave* their improper food, once they have a taste for it. Children want cheese and bread, but crave sweets. Wolfgang ought by rights to have his friends about him; he wants them even if without realizing it, but he *craves* admirers.

If it weren't bad for people to follow other people, Wolfgang's situation would be no harm to Rachel River, Minnesota, or wherever he is living. We have enough difficulty, however, overriding one hundred years of Scandinavian piety and the brutalization of the pioneer experience in order to find our own hearts and minds, without suddenly stunting this inner work by espying Wolfgang and taking him for our interpreter. The presence of anyone *special,* any leader figure, is bad for human beings trying to feel and think for themselves. Ernest Becker believed this so strongly that he thought Freud's major contribution was in pointing up our dangerous tendency to follow the leader.

I have two ideas for Minnesota towns who have artists and thinkers taking up residence; these ideas are directed to making any local gifted Wolfgang behave like a whole, vulnerable, judgeable person, no better or worse than ourselves.

First, never accept a gift from him *in his field*—but do accept a lot of gifts from him of physical work, committee work for the Business Development Association, scrubbing up after the county fair. If he writes a suite for St. Swithin's in the Swamp asking in return only that for heaven's sakes would the parish please remember in the Old Hundredth two beats on opening syllable and on each at the three end notes, pay him between $100 and $500 for the suite. Pay him $200 for the painting for the city hall, which you may or may not like. If you've paid for it you will find yourself able to say you don't like it and what's more the kids think that the whole bare white background with nothing but one vertical and one horizontal stripe looks like a flannel blanket pattern from Sears. People say that about Mondrian imitators on Fifty-seventh Street and at the Walker;

we can learn to say what we truly think in Rachel River, too. Further, being paid makes Wolfgang someone who gets hired like the rest of us. Our money is good enough for him. This will cut through the leader/prophet mystique. It will stop our getting a British class system, too. We don't want to end up always letting Mrs. the Hon. Someone cut the ribbon at the fête because her accent's O.K. One reason local Tories in England can be so poisonous is that they aren't paid directly for anything by the local people.

It is helpful to Wolfgang, too, not to feel that he is practicing *noblesse oblige* in his town. He cannot feed his "they don't know the value of my services here" illusion if he has been paid. This is also true of the relationship between clergymen and parish—usually a mucky one. It would be better for our countryside if we paid all clergymen a lot; then when they fail us in elevating the ancient symbols before us, and when they are too slothful to visit the sick or when they bore us, we can shout at them. That would be excellent for them and I would love it, personally. They have a lot to answer for, yet they hide behind their appalling salary level.

The other suggestion I have is that if we do Wolfgang any menial favors we make sure he does the same for us. Coming from the city as he does, he will have the habit of relating to other people in two distinct groups: those you care about, whom you call up, network style—and those who service your needs—repairmen and shopkeepers. This split is worse for human culture than we suppose. In the countryside we are pretty ingenious at keeping our communities together, but it means touching hand to boring and repetitive work. Wolfgang must do errands; he must drive for Meals on Wheels; he ought to meet a payroll; he ought to listen all the way through an Alanon meeting without raising his profile with one tiny creative peep.

We need to pay him, we need to give him two years to get over his urban habit of figuring his time for his own, we need to call him up ten times to help sandbag the Lac Qui Parle when it floods. What he lost with the Garden of Eden was being special and what we lost was being given spiritual guidelines by a leader. Both were probably good, not sad losses! Fourteenth-century priest and agricultural-labor leader John Ball insisted "When Adam delved, and Eve span—who was *then* the Gentleman?"

# The City Mouse,
# the Country Mouse, and the
# Overnight-Conference Mouse

---

*In cities men cannot be prevented from concerting together
and from awakening a mutual excitement which prompts
sudden and passionate resolution.*

—Alexis de Tocqueville

---

One beautiful noontime in 1941 my cousin and I were taken on
a picnic in the Piedmont of North Carolina. There was critical
illness in the family; an adult friend agreed to take us little
girls out of the way somewhere. We settled our picnic things
where new grass stood over the everlasting red clay, and an old
wooden mill, gray and winded, tottered over its brook. All the
way in the car a Mrs. Lowery told us children about rural values—the closeness to the earth that Carolina mountain people
feel, their natural courtesy, their stubborn acquaintance with
reality. Once we were settled, she sat on the blanket, leaned
against a tree, and prepared to enjoy the dogwoods. She pol-
ished some shards of mica in her smooth hands. We children
wanted nothing of that. We scrambled into the old mill, up its

treacherous ladder, and found a belfry. After a few good yanks we even got the bell going, and settled for some hard tolling until Mrs. Lowery called up to us sharply. She told us to enjoy Mother Nature. She pointed out Her beauties—the horizontal dogwood like cloud in the thin woods. The sky bloomed its soundless pale blue above us. The brook was spindling. Smothered in all this soundless, idle beauty, my cousin and I longed for love and hate: we looked for danger, any kind would do—a water moccasin, a copperhead. Then all three of us caught sight of an old, very poor man approaching. "You see, he is nearly like the earth itself," the sensitive Mrs. Lowery murmured to us. "Even his overalls—nearly the color of the sky."

"'Do, ma'am," he said to her, "'Do, miss; 'do, miss," to us. "I only came because I mind the bell was ringing five minutes ago."

"Oh, that!" Mrs. Lowery said in a cordial laugh to him. "That was just the children!"

He said, peering, "I thought maybe our country had won some great battle."

"Oh—we're not even at war yet," Mrs. Lowery said with a rich laugh.

"Not at war yet, ma'am," said the old man solemnly, getting it right.

"But our friends, the English, are having a bad time of it— they might get invaded," she went on.

The old man looked chastened. "Then our country is not at war."

The clever woman explained, with smiles, about Lend-Lease and U-boats—but the old man only stared at the mill bell. In dignity he stated, "Well, I'd thought our country might have won some great battle."

When he had gone Mrs. Lowery laughed. "O dear! O dear!" Gone, mysteriously, was the respect for earthy wisdom, the good mountain stock, gone in the laugh: "Some great battle indeed!" And the stupid southern sun shone on, on the woman's raillery, the children's longing for violence if violence was to be had, the old man's longing for heroic news.

This is the classic experience of the provinces: it is the swift undertow of Flaubert's understanding of provincial life—this feeling of being thousands of miles from where the *grande vie* is being lived. It is, in fact, still like that.

Whole trends of thought go by before they get to Montevideo and Madison. Death-and-dying hasn't got to Madison yet, although it is long passé in the Twin Cities. Stress, stages of life, midlife crisis, and holistic medicine have already followed, been lionized, and abandoned each in turn. Suburbs like St. Louis Park and Hopkins already had their Stepford Jungians before we out in the country stopped talking about "nerves." Out here we are still proclaiming, "You betcha! Doctor so-and-so doesn't fool around! He gave me enough broad-spec antibiotic to really knock it out!" Our social technology is early 1950s, our cultural fashion early 1960s, our religious life is 1549. That is all all right. The wonderful fields and groves never promised to make us *au courant*.

What is *not* all right is the limited and often hasty way in which the great world presents itself to us. The conferences that educators, humanists, and administrators get so many of we in the country get too few of. Regional Arts boards, the Countryside Council, the Farmers Union, and a few other organizations have started such conferences, but we need more. Most of us only get to the John Deere or International trips— and then you have to outsell half the country to win them.

One-evening conferences don't work at all, in my opinion. Four groups of people show up, their needs at odds. The groups are:

1. Public officials in related fields, attending on comp. time with mileage, who want above all a short evening of it. Half the time they privately know the group has been

convened only to meet the guidelines for citizen input, anyway, and that the real directives were drawn up months ago by Washington planners.

2. Volunteers, worn from their day's work, resenting the paid officials' gas allowances and comp. time, anxious to get hold of some Title Something funds or to initiate legislation. They want fast argument and means of leverage to change their environment. To them the leisurely remarks of Group 3 can be agonizing.

3. Senior citizens, who count on single-evening conferences for some of their social life. Public meetings provide them a format for wit, anecdote, and philosophy. Their pattern is not to take coffee throughout, as the public officials do; they wait until nine or nine-thirty, then they make a lunch occasion out of it. They frankly fall into light talk as they eat and drink, and it takes a gorilla of a moderator to gavel them out of it.

4. People with out-of-control agendas—those who erupt at public meetings. They use those convened as encounter group, support group, personal therapist, or parent. At any one-evening occasion, a moderator has to deal with them by promising to get back to them on that question (whatever it was) and then carefully keeping them from the floor. That saves the meeting for the others, but is grievous for the out-of-control agendist.

Overnight conferences serve all four groups better. The public officials can attend the first meeting, go home, and read the wrap-up later. The interested volunteers can corner the technocrats or administrators at coffee or drinks afterward. The seniors can count on the coffee hour to follow for genial, intelligent conversation. The out-of-control agendists can be talked to, and heard, by those present in the helping professions. They can be promised the later contacts they need. Their hearts' griefs will be somehow spoken to. They don't have to be psychological streakers to get attention. They will behave themselves at the next day's wrap-up.

I also propose that we divide up differently those funds which send people to overnight conferences. Professional people might halve the number they attend: farm and small-town people should quadruple the number they attend.

Out here, we would like to share in the intelligent talk. We want to get in on the trendy interpretations, as well—quite seriously. The tolling that the futurists hear is for us, too. We want to know if our country has won some great battle—or if humanity is losing one. I propose that the various merciful commissions and granting organizations of Minnesota somehow contrive to enable rural Minnesotans to go to two-day conferences to "concert together," as Tocqueville put it—so we all, rural as well as urban people, have a go at the "mutual awakening."

# The Sticking Place

In the countryside we get the point of normalcy. We garden happily. We sit on the farm stoop in the evenings. We know some body secrets which city people likely wouldn't guess, such as that the delicious, repairing thing to drink at noon during harvest is very hot coffee, not sugared cold drinks. Or when the field work is so hot one's eyes are sour with sweat and the body so exhausted at night that you stagger gingerly to the pickup, then the good thing is not the instant hot bath so dear to urbanites, but to sit on the ground and slowly dry and stiffen. I was disconcerted when this was first shown me. Then, in the 1960s, nutritionists explained that the sun's benefits have a chance to be absorbed when you don't bathe right away. So this sitting around dirty and fragile with tiredness was a sound instinct the whole while. Everyday virtues, everyday feelings, with no sharp changes, are our genius in the country.

When crisis comes, however, the personality must stagger to its feet, totter into the museum of bravery, find a suit of armor gone cold that looks as if it won't fit, and get it on, and rattle the fingers. The psychic equipment of everyday life—forbearance, patience—is no good now: we have to screw up our courage to a tougher sticking place. We have to become outspoken and decisive. To focus this problem, let us take the experience of firing a clergyman.

The urban equivalent of firing a clergyman is unknown to me but it must be something quite different, since whatever churches do or fail to do in the cities doesn't affect the whole community. Out here it does, however, and since our clergymen are so important, and visible, the really inadequate ones are that much more glaring. Occasionally, naturally, someone has to be fired. At least, every Minnesota town has had a clergyman who should have been fired, whether or not he in fact was. The main victims of this situation are the members of the call committee (hiring committee) who did their very best, loyally, endlessly, patiently, only in the end to hire an incompetent, slothful, sadistic, or crooked clergyman. When the truth came out the call committee felt awful, as though personally to blame. The weak-hearted members would choose to stand by the bad clergyman in an instinctive protection of their stake, so to speak. The strong-hearted ones would get the fellow fired and then feel *his* treachery and *their* guilt for months after.

I choose the firing of a clergyman because it involves a rural town in assessing and dismissing someone whose job is classier than most of ours are. Let us say we have determined, through congregational studies, that young people in trouble do not feel free to ask Pastor Kreven for help; married couples in difficulties would rather go to Spicer or Willmar (nearby towns with capable therapists) for expert psychological help than check in the pastor; welfare recipients are frightened of Pastor Kreven's evident distaste for the housekeeping level of their mobile homes; old people feel he might visit rather less seldom than he does; church council members feel that they patiently work out solutions to congregational problems in committee only to have their decisions overridden by the pastor; everyone agrees that man couldn't preach his way out of a wet paper bag, but no one would have asked for his resignation on that basis if it weren't for all the other disappointments in his serving them.

Despite all these complaints, despite his thoroughgoing incompetency on a dozen levels, he still represents a network of educated people far beyond the boundaries of the town. He has some support group out there whom we will never meet. Because those people are outside our town and outside our ken, we tend to be deluded into thinking they are closer to the intimidating powers-that-be than we are—they are part of the urban authorities who arrange things like Three Mile Island's venting of radioactive gases, and are responsible for all the other daunting news. If you figure that the world is made up of those who know how to get round a regulation or two and the others like us who have no connections, no clout, no say—then you can see how a clergyman, even a bent one with slovenly grammar, can appear to belong to the powers-that-be group. So we tend to be in awe of him.

Nearer to hand, our clergyman knows how to prevail in public—and in rural Minnesota anyone who can prevail in public has a great advantage over the dozens or hundreds of his flock. No matter how hilarious the party in the Fellowship Hall may be, when *he* says, "If you will please stand for the table prayer" we all obey. No one, not even a Patrick Henry among us if we have one, not even the conspirators trying to fire this man, would dream of saying genially, loudly, over everyone's heads: "Hold it just a second, will you, pastor? I want to finish telling Mahlon about the traveling salesman and the boa constrictor." We all fall silent. Obeying the man is normalcy, which we're good at. Firing him is a crisis, which we're not.

Since we need a stiffer stance for crisis than for normalcy, I would like to offer four ideas to achieve it. These ideas are not so much armor as four psychic muscles to exercise.

*First:* We must remind ourselves over and over of the difference between normalcy and crisis rather than denying it. A way to do this is to practice making distinctions. For example, the British presence in France was normal, St. Joan's response was critical. George III's colonial policies were normal, weren't they? Patrick Henry's and Samuel Adams's opposition was critical. Chamberlain tried to treat Hitler in the normal cause of statesmanship. Churchill recognized Hitler as the spearhead of a crisis. Marketing anything lucrative is normal, Dr. Kelsey's decision to keep thalidomide out of the United States was critical. Everyone can build his own distinctions, but the trick is to recognize the difference and be prepared to act forcefully in a scary or painful situation.

*Second:* We must forget the *background* of whatever the present evil is (wretched clergyman or whatever) and not look back to see who got us there. Crises almost without exception demand starting with this moment.

Let us, then, spare the poor call committee that brought Iago into our midst. I say this with feeling. I have served several times on hiring groups. In one of them I spoke in clarion tones against a certain applicant, pointing out how much time we'd all save if we admitted straight off that intuitively we all knew he was a bully. After a moment of delicious shock the other committee members looked gratified that someone had plainly said it and we moved on to the next applicant. Then, with my new-gained clout, I spoke in clarion tones for a certain well-qualified applicant who had a nice presence. Again people listened, and we hired this applicant. After her first month with us, during which she smoked pot all day and drank most of the night, she had so gummed up our operation you could scarcely find the typewriter erasers in the storeroom. It is terribly hard to hire people: one watches for this or that vice or virtue, and feels clever spotting it, and some monstrous thing gets right by us. So I am for deliberately forgetting who the call committee were.

*Third:* We have to use will power to remind ourselves constantly of the *invisible* people in the crisis—that is, those who will be hurt if we fail to take action. When one is in the midst of firing someone, one gets all tangled round with the feelings of the group right there, the feelings the poor fellow will have whom we are getting rid of, the immediate response of the press, and so on. It is easy to forget that the reason we are firing this person is that he has poorly served people who deserve better at his hands. If we fail to fire him, then it becomes we who have served them badly—insuring that their situation will not be improved. Since these people are not in the firing committee they are fairly invisible. Some of them are not born yet. If we keep this man on, those now ten years old will be badly counseled by him when they are teenagers; those now teenagers will be badly counseled by him when they are young married people; those now sixty will be neglected by him when they are seventy and would like a visitor.

Failure to picture those people makes a horrible liberal mush out of many groups convened to dismiss someone. One gets spaghetti-wrapped wth psychological tendrils like "We must consider, too, the effect this will have on his wife, who will feel that we are not dealing with her as Christians in one family"—and similar drivel.

*Fourth:* We must ask the local weekly newspapers to cover these fights. If justice wins out through citizen action, let's read about it and have our children read about it. If justice fails, let us bemoan it in print—and have our children read about the failure.

People need gossip, in any case, if only to feed our negative side. When the local papers report mostly positive, bland, normal events, we have to feed our gossip craving with our teenagers' reports of the girl who no sooner got to the prom than she just broke out all over her face. If there is newspaper coverage of a local crisis an important thing happens: the community begins to perceive itself in a genuine historical moment.

Rural people tend to think history takes place at My Lai, not here. They need to be reminded that genuine local history took place a decade and a half ago in the Utah countryside when Lewis Strauss's Atomic Energy Commission assured the people they had nothing to fear from underground testing. And genuine local history is taking place in Utah now. People are counting their leukemia cases. The old relaxing normalcy-loving slogan, "Oh, well—give him enough time—he'll hang himself!" won't do. It isn't itself that the AEC hanged.

It is so odd for us Minnesotans to be thinking of crisis, learning to gear up to it, when finally summer has come. Minnesota is beautiful. Skippers' wrists rest on small tillers on our thousands of lakes. Who wants to be paranoid? Surely Rachel Carson was just given to exaggeration.

# Growing Up Expressive

Love, death, the cruelty of power, and time's curve past the stars are what children want to look at. For convenience's sake, let's say these are the four most vitally touching things in life. Little children ask questions about them with relish. Children, provided they are still little enough, have no eye to doing any problem solving about love or death or injustice or the universe; they are simply interested. I've noticed that as we read aloud literature to them, about Baba Yaga, and Dr. Dolittle, and Ivan and the Firebird, and Rat and Mole, children are not only interested, they are prepared to be vitally touched by the great things of life. If you like the phrase, they are what some people call "being as a little child." Another way of looking at it is to say that in our minds we have two kinds of receptivity to life going on all the time: first, being vitally touched and enthusiastic (grateful, enraged, puzzled—but, at all events, *moved*) and, second, having a will to solve problems.

Our gritty society wants and therefore deliberately trains problem solvers, however, not mystics. We teach human beings to keep themselves conscious only of problems that *can* conceivably be solved. There must be no hopeless causes. Now this means that some subjects, of which death and sexual love come to mind straight off, should be kept at as low a level of consciousness as possible. Both resist problem solving. A single-minded problem solver focuses his consciousness, of course, on problems to be solved, but even he realizes there is a concentric, peripheral band of other material around the problems. This band appears to him as "issues." He is not interested in these issues for themselves; he sees them simply as impacting on the problems. He will allow us to talk of love, death, injustice, and eternity—he may even encourage us to do so because his group-dynamics training advises him to let us have our say, thus dissipating our willfulness—but his heart is circling, circling, looking for an opening to *wrap up* these "issues" so he can return attention to discrete, solvable problems. For example, a physician who has that mentality does not wish to be near dying patients very much. They are definitely not a solvable problem. If he is wicked, he will regard them as a present issue with impact on a future problem: then he will order experimentation done on them during their last weeks with us. It means his ethic is toward the healing process only, but not toward the dying person. His ethic is toward problem solving, not toward wonder. He will feel quite conscientious while doing the experiments on the dying patient, because he feels he is saving lives of future patients.

To return to little children for a second: they simply like to contemplate life and death. So our difficulty, in trying to educate adults so they will be balanced but enthusiastic, is to keep both streams going—the problem solving, which seems to be the mental genius of our species, and the fearless contemplation of gigantic things, the spiritual genius of our species.

The problem-solving mentality is inculcated no less in art and English classes than in mathematics and science. Its snake oil is hope of success: by setting very small topics in front of people, for which it is easy for them to see the goals, the problems, the solutions, their egos are not threatened. They feel hopeful of being effective. Therefore, to raise a generation of problem solvers, you encourage them to visit the county offices (as our sixth-grade teachers do) and you lead them to understand that this is citizenship. You carefully do not suggest that citizenship also means comparatively complex and hopeless activities like Amnesty International's pressure to get prisoners in far places released or at least no longer tortured. Small egos are threatened by huge, perhaps insoluble problems. Therefore, one feeds the small ego confidence by setting before it dozens and dozens of very simple situations. The ego is nourished by feeling it understands the relationship between the county recorder's office and the county treasurer's office; in later life, when young people find a couple of sticky places in county government, they will confidently work at smoothing them. How very different an experience such problem solving is from having put before one the spectacle of the United States' various stances and activities with respect to germ warfare. Educators regularly steer off all interest in national and international government to one side, constantly feeding our rural young people on questions to which one can hope for answers on a short timeline. We do not ask them to exercise that muscle which bears the weight of vast considerations—such as cruelty in large governments. By the time the average rural Minnesotan is eighteen, he or she expects to stay in cheerful places, devote some time to local government and civic work, and "win the little ones." Rural young people have a repertoire of pejorative language for hard causes: "opening that keg of worms," "no end to that once you get into it," "don't worry— you can't do anything about that from where you are," "we could go on about that forever!" They are right, of course: we could, and our species, at its most cultivated, does go on forever about love, death, power, time, the universe. But some of us, alas, have been conditioned by eighteen fashionably to despise those subjects because there are no immediate answers to all the questions they ask us.

The other way we negatively reinforce any philosophical bent in children is to pretend we don't see the content in their artwork. We comment only on the technique, in somewhat the same way you can scarcely get a comment on rural preachers' sermon content: the response is always, He does a good (or bad) job of speaking. "Well, but what did he say?" "Oh, he talked really well. The man can preach!"

The way to devalue the content of a child's painting is to say, "Wow, you sure can paint!" The average art teacher in Minnesota is at pains to find something to say to the third grader's painting of a space machine with complicated, presumably electronic equipment in it. Here is the drawing in words: A man is sitting at some controls. Outside his capsule, fire is flying from emission points on his ship toward another spaceship at right, hitting it. Explosions are coming out of its side and tail. What is an art teacher to do with this? Goodness knows. So he or she says, "My goodness, I can see there's a lot of action there!" It is said in a deliberately encouraging way but anyone can hear under the carefully supportive comment: "A lot of work going into nothing but more TV-inspired violence." One might as well have told the child, "Thank you for sharing."

I once attended a regional writers' group at which a young poet wrote about his feelings of being a single parent and trying to keep his sanity as he cared for his children. In his poem, he raced up the staircase, grabbed a gun, and shot the clock. When he finished reading it aloud to us, someone told him, "I certainly am glad you shared with us. I'd like to really thank you for sharing."

If we are truly serious about life we are going to have to stop thanking people for sharing. It isn't enough response to whatever has been offered. It is half ingenuous, and sometimes it is insincere, and often it is patronizing. It is the *dictum excrementi* of our decade.

I would like to keep in mind for a moment the art works described above: the child's painting of a spaceship assaulting another spaceship, and the harrowed father's racing up the staircase and shooting the clock. Here is a third. It is a twelve-year-old's theme for English class.

They were their four days and nights before anyone found them. It was wet and cold down there. As little kids at the orphanage, they had been beaten every night until they could scarcely make it to bed. Now they were older. Duane and Ellen leaned together. "I love you forever," she told him. He asked her, "Even though my face is marked from getting scarlett fever and polio and small pox and newmonya and they wouldn't take decent care of me, not call the doctor or anything, so the marks will always be on me?" "You know I love you," Ellen told him. "You know that time they tortured me for information and I was there but I didn't talk and later I found out it was your uncle who did it. I didn't talk because I remembered the American flag." Just then they heard someone shout, "Anyone alive down there in this mess?" You see a bomb had gone off destroying a entire U.S.A. city where they lived. Duane had lived with his cruel uncle who took him out of the orphanage to get cheap labor and Ellen lived at a boardinghouse where there were rats that ate pages of her diary all the time. Now they both looked up and shouted "We're here!" A head appeared at the top of the well into which they had fallen or they would of been in 6,500 pieces like all the other men and ladies even pregnant ones and little kids in that town. Now this head called down, "Oh—a boy and a girl!" then the head explained it was going for a ladder and ropes and it ducked away and where it had been they saw the beginnings of stars for that night, the stars still milky in front of the bright blue because the sky wasn't dark enough yet to show them up good.

The English teacher will typically comment on this story by observing that the spelling is uneven, and adjectives get used as adverbs. In rural Minnesota (if not elsewhere) an English teacher can spend every class hour on adjectives used as adverbs: it is meat and potatoes to a nag. But when we discuss spelling, syntax, and adverbs, we are talking method, not content. The child notices that nothing is said of the story's *plot*. No one remarks on the *feelings* in it. Now if this happens every time a child hands in fiction or a poem, the child will realize by the time he reaches twelfth grade that meaning or feelings are not worth anything, that "mechanics" (note the term) are all that matter.

It is rare for a public school English teacher to comment on a child's content unless the material is *factual*. Minnesota teachers encourage writing booklets about the state, themes on ecology and county government, on how Dad strikes the field each autumn, on how Mom avoids open-kettle canning because the USDA advises against it. In this way, our children are conditioned to regard writing as problem solving instead of contemplation, as routine thinking instead of imaginative inquiry.

How can we manage it otherwise?

I would like to suggest some questions we can ask children about their artwork which will encourage them to grow up into lovers, lobby supporters, and Amnesty International members, instead of only township officers and annual protestors against daylight saving time. Let us gather all the elements of the three artworks presented in this Letter: the little boy's spaceship-war painting, the young divorced father's narrative poem, and the twelve-year-old girl's story of love in a well. We have a set of images before us, then:

> Man directing spaceship fire
> Another aircraft being obliterated
> Staircase, man shooting a clock; children
> Cruel orphanage
> Torture
> Last survivors of a decimated city

Let us, instead of lending the great sneer to these images, be respectful of them. It may help to pretend the painting is by Picasso, that Flaubert wrote the father/clock scene, and that Tolstoy wrote the well story. It helps to remember that Picasso felt the assault of historical events on us—like Guernica; Flaubert, as skillfully as Dostoyevsky and with less self-pity, was an observer of violent detail; and the Tolstoy who wrote *Resurrection* or the scene of Pierre's imprisonment in *War and Peace* would turn to the well/love story without qualm.

We know we would never say to Picasso, Flaubert, or Tolstoy, "Why don't you draw something you know about from everyday life? Why don't you write about something you know about? You say Anna was smashed beneath a train? Thank you for sharing!"

The fact is that a child's feelings about orphanages and torture and love are things that he does know about. They are psychic realities inside him, and when he draws them, he is drawing something from everyday life. Sometimes they are from his night life of dreaming, but in any event they are images of passion and he is drawing from his genuine if garbled experience. A few years ago there was a stupid movement to discourage children's reading of Grimms' fairy tales. Later, with a more sophisticated psychology, we learned that the stepmother who is hostile and overweening is a reality to all children; the cutting-off of the hero's right hand and replacing of it with a hand of silver is a reality to all children. Spaceships, witches' gingerbread houses, orphanages, being the last two people to survive on earth—all these are part of the inner landscape, something children know about. Therefore, in examining their artwork, we need better sets of questions to ask them. Young people who are not repressed are going to lay their wild stuff in front of adults (hoping for comment of some kind, praise if possible) until the sands of life are run, so we had better try to be good at responding to them. And unless we want to raise drones suitable only for conveyor-belt shifts, we had better be at least half as enthusiastic as when they tell us, Mama, I got the mowing finished.

Here are some questions to ask our young artist. How much of that electronic equipment is used for firepower and how much just to run the ship? After the other spaceship is blown up and the people in it are dead, what will this man do? Will he go home somewhere? Were the stars out that night? You said he'll go home to his parents. Did the other man have parents? How soon will that man's parents find out that his spaceship was destroyed? Could you draw in the stars? You said they were out—could you draw them into the picture some way? but don't ruin anything you've got in there now. Also, that wire you said ran to the solar plates, will you darken it so it shows better? Don't change it—just make it clearer. Yes—terrific! Can you see the planet where the other man would have returned to if he had lived till morning?

*The young father's story:* There is an obvious psychic complication to this story: the violence in his shooting out the clock face is gratuitous, and the plea for attention on the part of the author directed at the reader is glaring: clock faces as psychological symbols are in the public domain. Anyone who tells a friend (or a group of strangers) I am going to shoot up a clock face at 11 P.M. is asking for psychological attention. In a civil world, to ask is to receive, so if we are civilized we have to pay attention and ask the young author: Why does the father in the story blast the clock? And, when he replies, we have to ask some more. If there was ever an instance in which it was O.K. to say, "Thanks for sharing," this is not it.

I should like to add that this will be especially difficult for rural teachers because the traditional country way to treat any kind of mental problem is to stare it down. It didn't happen. I didn't hear that insane thing you just said, and you know you don't really hate your mother. What nice parent would shoot a clock? We uniformly do what Dr. Vaillant in *Adaptations to Life* would call a denial adaptation. It takes a brave questioner when the young person brings in a crazy story.

*The well/love story:* Did you know there really are such orphanages? There are orphanages where the children have to get up at four-thirty to work in the dairy, and the girls work hours and hours in the kitchens, and the children's growth is stunted. Did you make the girl so brave on purpose? Were they a lucky couple or an unlucky couple, or is that the sort of a question you can't ask? You made a point of telling us they'd been through a lot of hardship. What would it have been like for them if they hadn't? Do you want to talk about what blew up the city? Did you imagine yourself in the well?

Those are not brilliant questions; they are simply respectful, because the art works described are concerned with death by violence; cruelty by institutions; treachery by relations; bravery (or cowardice—either one is important); sexual love, either despite or encouraged by dreadful circumstances.

They are some of the subjects in *War and Peace*, in Dürer's etchings, paintings, and woodcuts, and in *Madame Bovary*.

It is a moot question in my mind which of two disciplines will be the more useful in helping people stay vitally touched by the Great Things: psychology might do it—and English literature in high school might do it (instruction on the college level is generally so dutiful to methodology that it seems a lost cause to me. "How did D. H. Lawrence foreshadow this event?" and "What metaphors does Harold Rosenberg use in his discussion of Action Painting?" are the questions of technocrats, not preservers of spirit. It is as if we got home from church and the others said, "How was church?" "We had Eucharist," we tell them. "Well, how was it?" they ask. "Pretty good," we reply. "Bishop Anderson was there. He held the chalice eight inches above the rail so no one spilled, then he turned and wiped the chalice after each use so no germs were passed along. People who had already communed returned to their benches using the north aisle so there was no bottlenecking at the chancel.")

I don't think churches will be helpful in preserving the mystical outlook as long as they see life and death as a *problem*—a problem of salvation—with a solution to be worked at. Churches have an axe to grind. They might take the father running up the staircase to be an impact subject: they would wish to use their program to solve his problem. Churchmen often appear to be companionable counselors, but the appearance is largely manner and habit. Under the manner, the clergyman's mindset is nearly always to see a disturbed or grieving person's imagery as *the issues*. From there, he swings into psychological problem solving.

I would like to commend this responsibility to our English teachers: that they help our children preserve pity, happiness, and grief inside themselves. They can enhance those feelings by having young children both write and draw pictures. They can be very enthusiastic about the children's first drawings of death in the sky. Adults, particularly mature ones who have *not* got children in school at the moment, should make it clear that we expect this of English teachers and that we don't give a damn if LeRoy and Merv never in their lives get the sentence balance of past conditional and perfect subjunctive clauses right. We need to protect some of the Things Invisible inside LeRoy and Merv and the rest of us.

This is my last Letter from the Country. That is why it is so shrill. Gadflies are always looking out a chance to be shrill anyway, so I jumped to this one and have shouted my favorite hope: that we can educate children not to be problem solvers but to be madly expressive all their lives.